# *MoMoirs.*
# *I'll give you something to cry about!*

## *Introduction*

Think of MoMoirs as literary apron strings. A MoMoir is a way of holding on to your children long after you've actually let them go; of remembering and recapturing your mother and your relationship with her.

The whole idea for MoMoirs came about when my daughter Charlotte casually announced that she had 209 days left before she got her driver's license. How could that be? She had just recently learned to walk. How could she suddenly be old enough to drive? Where had the time gone? That was the day I came up with the MoMoirs concept…a way of capturing my daughter and my feelings about her before she literally drove out of my life. I kept a daily journal for the next six months. It allowed me to indelibly engrave my daughter in my mind.

I introduced the MoMoirs workshop to my three friends. We met nearly every week for two years.

The workshop involved us responding to prompts, both verbal and visual to spark memories. Topics like birth, footwear, absent fathers, bad habits, favorite food, invasion of privacy. Often, we spent more time talking which actually helped the writing process. Even those of us who had never written before began to deeply appreciate what capturing these memories of our departed mothers and now grown children on paper truly meant. Writing, rewriting, polishing, editing and tweaking.

Our backgrounds are all very different but so many of our experiences and emotions were the same. The pieces you'll find in this book are just a random selection of the many we wrote. The stories we share here are needless to say all fact not fiction. They're about us, our mothers and our children, our pain and our deepest joys. We hope this collection of writing gives you something to cry about, laugh with and enjoy.

Linda Howard Urbach

October, 2013

# Ten Stories by Gayle Gleckler

*Don't Go Out Of The House Without Your Underwear*

*The Daddy Sickness*

*Sensible Shoes*

*Not Well Suited*

*On The Road Again*

*Start The Day With A Bad Breakfast*

*First Daddy, Second Chance*

*Whoops*

*The Verdict*

*Measured In Inches*

*Me, age three with my underwear on.*

# Don't Go Out Of The House Without Your Underwear

## Age 3

I was three and the day was a bright shiny sparkler in July. It started out so beautifully with a real all-American breakfast replete with all the right colors, smells, and ingredients. It was very well balanced. We were just pretending to be. You see, that was before my Daddy left us for another woman. My Daddy Alex was Daddy Number One. He and Mommy adopted me. I didn't realize until many years later adopting someone is actually more of a commitment in many ways than having a biological baby. But Daddy Number One left us anyway. I guess she made better breakfasts.

We lived in a perfect white center-hall Colonial house with a perfect white picket fence, and we grew perfect beefsteak tomatoes. To this day tomatoes are my favorite food and beef, my second. Pretending to be perfect, we were nestled in the middle of the country in Upper Arlington, the poshest suburb of Columbus, Ohio.

Mommy had warned me many times: "Gayle, don't go out of the house without your underwear."

But the inner child in me asked, "Why not? It feels so good." A natural-born risk taker and devilishly defiant, I played life on the edge of the yard. I ventured out into the fresh Ohio air, which blew up my multicolored polka-dotted pinafore that resembled a Wonder Bread wrapper. The fresh wind playfully swirled up my skirt, refreshing all my unimprisoned baby girl parts. I was not to be encumbered or dragged down by pesky underpants. Not me.

On this perfect Ohio day, Mommy had gotten me a very special treat: a hot pink plastic bottle filled with bubbly sparkling liquid. When I unscrewed the lid, there was a surprise inside, a silver stick with a hollow circular silver ring at the end. Mommy instructed me to dip the ring inside the bubbly shininess and scoop out some of the gooey liquid that clung to the ring.

Then she said, "Blow. Blow it out, Gayle."

I did, and like magic, three rainbow-colored bubbles flew out beautifully silhouetted against the vibrant blue sky. They glistened like my vibrantly perfect life. They were perfectly round and I had created them all by myself with my baby-sweet, unpantied breath.

I was very proud of myself and quite confident since my first attempt was so successful, so I joyfully dipped the ring again into the pink liquid. But I forgot the basic rule: instead of powerfully blowing it out, I exuberantly sucked it in.

Oh no. Ouch. Sting. Ouch. My perfect day was fading fast. My throat was burning, and my tongue felt as if it were curling into a nasty tunnel. My lips were a five-alarm fire. I screamed bloody murder and learned a big lesson that day that burst my baby bubbles. Bubbles are meant to be blown out, and when you inhale them, it sucks.

Mommy took me by the hand and dragged me screaming into our perfect house. I kept crying until she soothed my seared mouth and crushed ego by washing away the soapy stuff with cool water, then with refreshing apple juice.

Not to be daunted on such a beautiful Buckeye day by the bubble-sucking setback, I ventured out of the house again without my you-know-whats and renewed enthusiasm. Within minutes it happened, something I never could have imagined. A yellow jacket flew fearlessly up my flowing pinafore and without a second thought stung me on my second set of lips.

This time I bellowed so loudly, it made the unfortunate bubble incident seem like a summer whisper. These pink lips were even more tender. But I was deeply confused between expressing immense pain and feeling immensely guilty. I knew Mommy would be even more furious with me.

Mommy scooped me up and carried me into our so far still perfect house. She gingerly applied Mercurochrome to my "down there" lips. Then came the predictably firm words: "Gayle, how many times have I told you not to go out of the house without your underwear?"

I cried and cried. What began as a perfect day had gone seriously downhill and turned tragic in my three-year-old existence. Later in life I discovered that was not the first time I was to have my bubbles burst or get burned on both sets of lips. A bit of innocence lost. A bit of wisdom gained.

To this day I always blow out, not in, and I never go out of the house without my underwear. Plus, my underwear is always lacy, pretty, and very clean, just in case I get into an accident. I also instinctively steer clear of any man who's wearing a yellow jacket.

*Proper Mom Romaine making sure my underwear is on!*

My adoptive parents, Romaine and Alex Gleckler were married in Columbus, Ohio in 1938.

# The Daddy Sickness

## Age 3

"Mommy, why are we here again?"

"Gayle, we are in Hartford, Connecticut. We've just rented this apartment with furniture already in it for a month to see if Daddy is going to get a great new job in mortgage banking right here in Hartford. He's just trying it out for a month to see if he likes the job and if the people at the bank like Daddy."

"Who wouldn't like Daddy? But if they like him too much, does that mean we have to move here from Ohio?"

"Yes, honey."

"Mommy, my throat really hurts, especially when I swallow."

"I'm sorry, sweetie; let me make you some hot cocoa. It will soothe your sore throat and make it feel better."

I drank her steamy offering of a cup of calmness.

"See? Doesn't your throat feel better now?"

"A little bit, but not if we move here. Mommy, do I have to give up my beautiful pink, lacy bedroom? Can we move it here?"

"Well, no, we can't move your exact bedroom here, but we can bring all the beautiful things you love in your bedroom right here to Hartford."

"Mommy, I feel like I'm going to throw up.".

"Okay, hold on; let's go to the bathroom."

We ran to the strange old bathroom. Mommy held my head by my forehead as I knelt on the cold black-and-white checkered tile floor and bent awkwardly over the looming white toilet bowl. Her holding my head was somehow comforting.

As I will I learn later in life, when you are older and throw up, no one will be there to hold your head. I heaved up the hot chocolate and anything else that had been hanging around in my tummy for the past twenty-four hours. Afterward Mommy washed my mouth out with cold water, and I brushed my teeth to get rid of the acrid taste and odor. She held my hand as we walked back to the foreign living room with the funny-smelling, plum-colored flowered couch. I lay down with my head in her lap, as she put a cool washcloth on my forehead.

"Honey, I need to take your temperature."

She went back to the rented bathroom and reappeared with a threatening glass thermometer with a red liquid center.

"Now, relax, honey, and let me take your temperature. Lift up your tongue." She inserted the ice-cold thermometer into my reluctant mouth. My tongue sank it into a precarious yet secure position. I was scared. I choked. I've always had a quick gag reflex.

After a few minutes Mommy removed the instrument of tongue torture and looked at the height of the ominous red line.

"Oh my, Gayle, you have a 101-degree fever."

We heard Daddy's wing-tipped shoes clumping up the rickety staircase to our dismally furnished temporary second-floor apartment.

"Here's Daddy, Gayle. Daddy's coming home from work."

The old wooden stairs complained, creaking from weary wear, as he opened the door with his huge, welcoming, warm, super-white smile.

My heart leapt up at the handsome presence of his Daddiness. I jumped up, momentarily cured as I was wrapped in the comfort of his strong, engulfing, comfortable, muscled arms. I smelled his Old Spice aftershave and got dizzy from his Daddy love aroma.

"How's my best, prettiest girl ever?" he asked, smothering me in Daddy kisses. "Daddy, Daddy, do we have to move here? I don't want to. I love Ohio. I love my

friends. I love my pink bedroom with all my stuffed animals."

"We'll see, but before we talk about that sweetie, let me feel your forehead. Mommy says you are sick." He gently touched my forehead with his cooling hand. "Romaine, she's burning up," he said to my mother with admonishment.

"I know; she has been all day," said Mom.

I threw up again.  No dinner for me. I finally fell fitfully to sleep. The next day was pretty much a rerun of the day before.

The next night we heard Daddy's car roaring up the gravel-paved driveway. The engine stopped. There it was, that "Daddy's home" sound I had learned to rely on night after night. I was like Pavlov's puppy, salivating at just the anticipation of his entrance. Even here in this strange town the Daddiness feeling was consistent. Same Daddy, look, and smell—and he  was all mine.

"Hi, Daddy. Daddy, my throat still really hurts."

Mommy said, "Alex, I don't think Gayle is getting any better."

"You'd better take her to a doctor tomorrow. What's her temperature now?" "It's still 101."

I fell asleep, tossing and turning feverishly. But in a haze I heard them talking, and it didn't sound good. Not at all good.

The next night Daddy came home much later. Mommy and I already eaten dinner, my get-better-or-else chicken soup, before he got home. This was not normal. I still couldn't keep food down and my throat was ablaze. I walked out into the non-living room, surprising them with my sudden presence.

"Daddy, do we really have to move here? I love Ohio."

Mommy said, "No, Gayle, we have something to tell you."

She paused, looked at Daddy, then at me and said quietly, "Daddy's been working in the office on trial to see if he's suited for it. As it turns out, he is. So Daddy's going to accept the new job, a great opportunity for him, and you and I are going to stay in Ohio. Daddy's going to live here most of the time and come home some of the time."

"I don't understand. Does that mean we aren't going to live together? We always live together, don't we?"

"I understand how you feel, but Daddy and I have decided it's better if we don't live together. It's better if we live apart."

"But we are supposed to live together, Mommy and Daddy and Gayle. That's how we know how to live. Are you getting a divorce?"

"We'll talk about that later, honey."

I knew on some child level that that must mean yes. I started to cry and went into the bathroom to be alone, pretending to throw up with no hand holding my head. An hour later my temperature was now 102. I was burning up and crying up. And I had just learned an amazing lesson.

Getting sick will not keep the man you love the most in the world from leaving you. That night I hugged Daddy harder than I had ever hugged him, not wanting to ever let him go, and cried even harder.

Then I went  into the bathroom and threw up everything inside me—especially my heart.

*On the beach with my Dad, circa 1946.*

*Daddy and I loved each other so much. 1945.*

*Mom and me in sensible shoes, 1948.*

# Sensible Shoes

### Age 6

My five foot nine mother always strutted around in three-inch-high heels, making her six feet tall presence always intimidating. Sexy. Glamorous. All the time. So why did I have to wear ugly sensible shoes like Buster Browns? In 1949 we lived in Columbus, Ohio, where the totally hummable, catchy "Buster Brown" jingle would sing out of the cloth-mouthed, round-topped mahogany Zenith radio:

I'm Buster Brown,

I live in a shoe.

That's My my dog Tide.

He lives in there, too.

Whoever thought that one up was nuts. Who would name a dog Tide? Was he super-clean because he was washed with Tide or dumb enough and small enough to live inside a smelly old shoe?

It was September, that dreaded yet somewhat anticipatory and exciting "Back to School" time. I was entering second grade and feeling rather full of myself, having survived first grade with straight O's for Outstanding. Getting ready for school meant going through the excruciating experience of shopping with my always frugal mother. Frugal is just not a quality one desires in a fellow shopper.

"Back to School" shoes were solidly classified in the sensible category and, of course, in the sensible color, brown, with the shoelaces in the perfect accent color, "never show dirt" brown. When it came to sensible shoes, no one did it better than Buster Brown, with its über-ugly lace-up clunkers.

Mom and I determinedly walked into the very sensible shoe store. The middle-aged, potbellied, overly pleasant sensible salesman asked, using a falsely interested tone, "And what's your name, young lady?"

"Gayle," I said glumly.

"What style are you interested in?"

My mind was screaming, "None of these, Buster. I want sexy high heels like Mom." Before I could blurt out my wish, however, my mother ever so predictably jumped in, "We want something sensible for "Back to School" shoes, like Buster Browns."

And I'm thinking, "No, we don't!"

"And what's your size, Gayle?"

"Not sure. I think my feet grew over the summer." Mom said, "I think she's a six."

I was probably a five, but I was on to her motives. She wanted to buy a size larger so I would quote, unquote, "grow into them." But the real reason was, we didn't have much money on her single-mom's salary. I knew the spendthrift drill by heart. If we polished these new shoes often enough, they would last until next year's dreaded "Back to School" shoe purchase.

The nice phony salesman disappeared into the back room, returning with two shoe boxes decorated with the Buster Brown logo. Buster Brown was tightly hugging his dog. They looked extremely happy. I was not. The tissue paper in the boxes rustled as the salesman reached inside to grab the size five Buster Brown to put on my left foot and a size six to put on my right. Now, where was that dog when I really needed him to bite this guy's hairy hand as he slipped my teeny-weeny tootsies into these hideous big brown boats?

Now came the fun part, the moment I'd been waiting for: the sizing of my too-small feet in these too-large shoes using scary but exciting x-rays. Together the salesman and I strolled over to the green x-ray machine.

I tried to act nonchalant as I stepped up to the ominous-looking machine, which came up to the top of my chest. I was barely tall enough to peer in. I stealthily slipped my feet into the eerie cave holes, which instantly swallowed them up. Like in a Captain Marvel comic book, my feet mysteriously disappeared inside to even more magically reappear at the top in an alien chartreuse green color. I wiggled my toes inside my left size five and then my toes inside the size six. I found this terribly amusing, especially since Mom and the salesman were terminally serious. My mother scrunched down next to me, head to head, to gaze in too. Then she swapped places with the annoyingly ingratiating salesman, whose head I didn't want next to mine. Like a shoe doctor, he carefully examined my skeletal green feet in the Buster Browns. The point of this x-ray exercise was to see exactly how far my toes were from the tip of the shoe. Then we could make an educated guess as to what size to purchase.

Infuriatingly predictably, my mom said, "Oh, I think the size six looks much better, don't you, sir? It gives her room to grow into them."

Salivating to make this "Back to School" sale, he eagerly agreed, placating Mom, the Buster Brown purchase-paying person.

"Oh, yes, ma'am, I think the size six fits her much better and gives her that all-important room to grow into in the future."

I wondered if he got more money on the sale if he sold us the larger size.

Mom and I left the sensible store with my new Buster Browns in a sensible bag and headed for our special mom-and-daughter treat, which always made me happy. But mostly I was ecstatic that the sensible ordeal was behind us. We went to the corner Walgreen's drugstore and did something I always loved. We sat at the counter on the red leather stools that were so high my feet dangled freely, not touching the floor. There was a gorgeous blonde, who looked like Sandra Dee, gazing down at me from a poster faded to a light green from too much sun exposure. As if to tease or mock me, she was wearing alluring three-inch-high heels. I swore someday that would be me in her sexy red shoes.

We ordered our favorite, an open hot roast beef sandwich surrounded by a mound of mashed potatoes with a crater filled with brown gravy that matched my new shoes. I also ordered a fizzy Cherry Coke, and Mom and I split a mountainous banana split oozing with hot fudge and real whipped cream with a cherry on top. As we headed home, I was enjoying a delicious sugar high, fantasizing that Tide would jump out of my bag when we got home to my girly pink bedroom. I secretly wanted to steal Tide away from Buster Brown and have him as my own darling puppy to live with us forever, and not just inside my shoe.

In retrospect, the only thing that was not sensible was the green x-ray machine. One day they all just mysteriously vanished. Their disappearance was never explained to me, but I was left with a strange, uneasy feeling that the fun green x-ray machine either made me sterile or gave me cancer. But how could I question the wisdom of adults, especially my mother? It was, after all, the sensible thing to do.

**Some Thirty Years Later**

I learned a few things. First of all, the dog inside the Buster Brown shoes was not named Tide. As strange as Tide was, his real name was actually weirder. It was Tige. And the foot-to-shoe measuring devices I believed to be green x-ray machines were actually fluoroscopes. There was a rash of cases of thyroid cancer in the Midwest years later, most heavily concentrated in Ohio. The cancer was supposedly linked to the now extinct machines that are probably emitting an eerie green glow in a landfill somewhere near Columbus, Ohio.

Once I moved to Manhattan after college, I never wore flats or brown shoes again. And as it turned out, I wasn't sterile. When my son, Zac, was two, I strolled with him in Chelsea one day wearing my $600 Susan Bennis and Warren Edwards' spikes. They were all the rage—turquoise snakeskin, open-toed slingbacks—and as far from sensible as shoes could possibly be. We approached Space Kiddets, the poshest children's clothing store in chic Chelsea. It was then I spied them, the most adorable high-topped sneakers I had ever seen. They were multicolored: red, blue, yellow, green, and turquoise. The left sneaker had red laces, the right, yellow. We left with those $60 sneakers on Zac's sweet feet, which he would most certainly outgrow in six months.

Sensible, Be Damned!

I strutted down the street to meet my husband (who wore nothing but the coolest soft leather Italian loafers) at Positano's, the most "in" restaurant of the moment. Zac sat with us eating spaghetti and was fascinated as he stared mesmerized at his new rainbow-colored shoes.

*A Footnote:*

*I've learned we either become our mother or turn sharply on our three-inch stilettos and run as far as possible in the opposite direction.*

*Mom in her high heels, my whole life!*

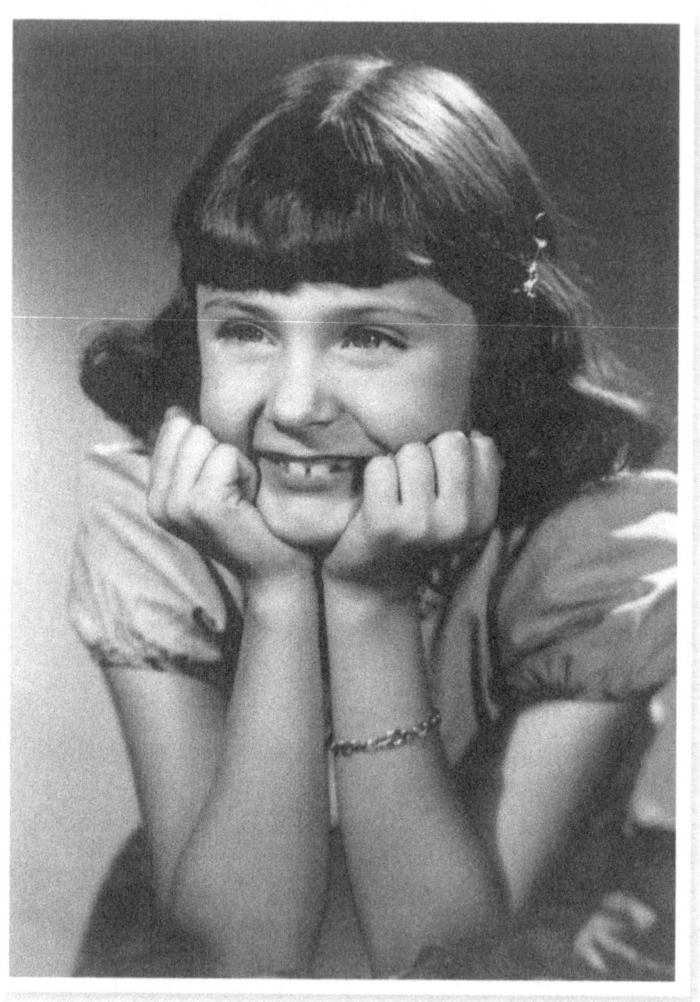

*Me at age seven hardly starving.*

# Start The Day
# With A Bad Breakfast

Age 7

To say my mother couldn't boil an egg would be unfair, but to say she couldn't fry one would be more than fair. My school days were her workdays, so Monday through Friday breakfasts were so forgettable I can barely remember them. But I'm guessing everyday started with cereal, either Grape Nuts, which was like chewing through cement droppings, or a big bowl of the Snap, Crackle, and Pop of America's favorite, Rice Krispies.

Saturday morning was quite different. As the only child of a single working mom, which was very rare in those days, we did the chores. This meant a rushed breakfast before we did the wash, changed the beds and towels, vacuumed with our trusty stand-up Hoover, and scrubbed, or as we said in Ohio, scoured the bathroom floor, tub, and toilet. This all had to be done before I was allowed to go out and play. Oh, how I hated Saturday mornings!

Ah, but Sunday. Sunday was "The Real Breakfast" day. This breakfast was a prelude to our Presbyterian church service with its boring Sunday school, where the only thing I liked was coloring Jesus either in the manger or on the cross. He always seemed to be being born or dying.

The tension was high in the kitchen. Mom would start frying the bacon. The kitchen almost burst with the mouthwatering, misleading aroma not fairly forecasting the bad texture ahead. You see, Mom, being born and raised in Ohio, did what her mother did before her and her mother before her: she cooked the trichinosis out of everything whether it needed it or not. Even our broccoli was in no danger of transmitting the dreaded pork offender. So the bacon shrank, curling in agony to half its size, as it was burned to death beyond crispy recognition. But trust me, it had no trichinosis.

For my mother, the complex coordination of the various breakfast parts was a totally nerve-racking ordeal. This was long before the word *multitasking* existed. To aid in the campaign, I was assigned to set the table perfectly with the required meticulous napkin folding. Next, I poured the dreadful acidic, tinny-tasting canned orange juice into glasses decorated with hand-painted cheery red cherries supported by perky green stems. The Folgers coffee would happily hiss as it brewed in the bubbling glass percolator. The toast responsibility was mine—the pièce de résistance. The soft, squishy white Wonder Bread, with my gentle coaxing, nestled neatly into our antique two-slice toaster with its badly drawn rose etched on one side. This toaster had a mind of its own. The toast popped up whether it was done or not. Usually it was not, so back it went to toast hell. Then, as you probably guessed, it exhaustedly popped up overdone, in a burnt amber hue to perfectly accessorize the shrunken, defeated bacon that had resigned itself to being the same unappetizing color.

Then the dreaded egg carton came out. The real power struggle was about to begin. Which came first, Mom or the egg?

Sizzling Crisco was expectantly lying in wait in the scuffed up aluminum frying pan, which heroically wore the battle scars from previous "Mommy" scorchings. Some bursts of splatter would be heard when the first egg was cracked into the pan. Splat. A broken yellow death. The yolky fireworks were about to commence.

Mom would explode with the first yolk down: "Damn egg!"

The next egg actually made it into the frying pan safely, but at the very first nudge of the spatula—you guessed it—there was another death in the yellow maze. Mom's anxiety level would rise swiftly with every egg abortion. She broke into a severe breakfast sweat.

"Goddamn these eggs. A bad batch, a rotten dirty dozen!"

The third egg proceeded to bite the pan, then the fourth splat into the fryer. It would begin to look like a Jackson Pollock painting gone horribly wrong in the skillet.

"Gayle, damn it. Butter the toast."

By now the forgotten Wonder bread toast had lost its purpose. I cut little squares of cold butter, which were stubbornly not about to melt out of protest from gross neglect. The lost little Wonder slices were obviously as mad at me as Mom apparently was.

"Gayle, get the plates. Get the bacon. Get the toast."

I can't help but think what she really wanted to say was, "Gayle, get lost."

Oh yes, breakfast in Ohio with Mom was a total delight. As her anxiety rose to great unculinary heights, my appetite plummeted. Serenity and breakfast with Mom were an impossibility. To say I had lost my desire for eating would be an understatement.

Today I always skip breakfast. But go figure? I just love to cook it. But only on Sunday. And I always call it brunch.

A ROMANTIC CRUISE ended here Saturday for Mrs. Romaine Gleckler who came to Honolulu for her marriage this week to Charles L. Baker. The Columbus, Ohio, woman was accompanied by her daughter, Gayle, of a former marriage, and Paul Budd. Mr. Budd will serve as best man for Mr. Baker at the wedding which is scheduled for Thursday. Mrs. Gleckler will be at the Islander hotel until after the wedding.—Star-Bulletin photo.

*Mom and me marry our next husband in Hawaii.*

# Not Well Suited

## Age 8

I was eight. I was in third grade. Mom said, "Gayle, I got a letter from Uncle Bake." Uncle Bake looked like a movie star, Van Johnson to be exact.

The letter, simplified in my memory many years later, read:

*Dear Romaine and Gayle,*

*You know I love you both dearly, so what I'm proposing is marriage. I think the three of us will be very happy together. I would love to have you both move here to Honolulu, Hawaii, and live with me in paradise. I think you will both love it as I do. I have a perfect three-bedroom ranch-style white house just two blocks from the most glorious white sand beach and aqua ocean. Please sell the house in Bexley, Ohio [a suburb of Columbus] and come here and live with me in the most beautiful place imaginable. I have made some wonderful friends who you will really enjoy. Please come.*

*Love, Bake*

After reading the letter to me while I was tucked into bed, huddled in my flannel pajamas, Mom asked, "Well, Gayle, what do you think?"

Now, let me ask you. If you were eight in a freezing cold, boring, gray Columbus, Ohio, and hated your third-grade teacher, what would you say? I was more than ready to bid snowmen goodbye.

After thinking about it for what must have seemed like an eternity to Mom but was probably one minute, I responded, "Yes, Mom, please! Let's move to Hawaii."

As it turned out to be true of most of my life, my motivation wasn't so much driven by my desire to go to a new destination, as it was fueled by my need to get out of the situation I was in.

"Gayle, are you sure you mean it? You really want to move?" "Yes, yes, I really mean it. Let's go. How soon?"

"Okay, I'll tell Uncle Bake yes."

The Hawaiian arrangements moved very quickly. Mom didn't let any grass skirts grow under her feet.

So with great haste we sold our charming gray Victorian house on Montrose Avenue, and Mom purchased plane tickets to San Francisco.

The flight was thrilling. This was during the 1950's, when you dressed up to fly cross-country, or anywhere, for that matter. The TWA stewardesses were so beautiful they looked like the movie stars on the covers of Silver Screen, my favorite magazine.

After our flight we spent a couple of days sightseeing and shopping in the magical hilly city. Then we boarded the extremely luxurious Lurline cruise ship to cross the Pacific and come to dock in paradise.

The ship was elegant, sophisticated in design, and had sumptuous bountiful meals all of which I soon threw up. Except for the distraction of my atrocious seasickness, my delirious tropical fantasies went wild. All I could imagine was trading in my ballet tutu for a grass skirt, doing the hula, and living in a hut on the beach.

But the most exciting expectation for me was what we brought with us in our suitcases. Before we left Ohio, Mom and I had gone to a tailor. I had never had something specially made for me, just for me, to fit only me. The tailor made Mom and me matching wedding suits, tightly fitted at the waist, created from robin's egg blue silk. Our elegant nuptial suits fit us like second-skin gloves.

Together we looked like a most anticipatory, eligible, adorable wedding pair, mother and daughter mail-order brides.

We cruised into the breathtaking Honolulu harbor, and it was indeed paradise. The intoxicating scents alone were enough to send me to olfactory heaven. Friendly sepia-skinned natives covered us in leis. The fragrant white gardenias were my favorite. Ukuleles hummed in unison as our greeters sang Hawaiian songs to welcome us. The hula dancers twirled and swished their sensual dried palms all around us. Uncle Bake gave us hugs and kisses. I was indeed in heaven.

The next day my mother and I had the most wonderful wedding in our matching matrimonial blue silk suits as "We" married handsome, charming Uncle Bake who became Daddy Number Two. The three of us were just the picture of a perfect family, except for one small detail: not only did Uncle Bake look like Van Johnson, he was gay like Van Johnson.

I was too young to know what "gay" was. I thought it meant happy. And Uncle Bake looked so hunky in his U.S. Army uniform, the so anti-gay Army. This was way before "Don't Ask, Don't Tell."

It was more like "Never tell, or I'll kill you."

So Mom and I, dressed like perfect fems, were cast as his beards. It wasn't until I was fourteen that I found out Uncle Bake was gay. It wasn't until I was twenty-two that I found out what a beard was.

But the good news is because of "Us" marrying gay Bake, I am now a very creative cook, can do a drop-dead floral arrangement, and can attempt a passable hula fueled with enough champagne.

Mom was big on proverbs, so marrying Uncle Bake might have been a "Bird in the hand is worth two in the bush," although I can pretty well guess he was never in the bush.

SATURDAY'S LURLINE BROUGHT MRS. ROMAINE DOWNIN GLECKLER, bride to be of Charles L. Baker. They will be marrie December 21 and plan to live in Kailua. She has been in the publ relations office of Capital university in Columbus, O., as alumni secre ary. Mr. Baker, an employe of M. McInerny, attended West Virgin niversity and the University of Virginia.

*Mom's glamorous wedding announcement, very Barbara Stanwick.*

*Charles Baker, Daddy #2, stationed in Pearl Harbor, Hawaii.*

# On The Road Again

### Age 10

Hey, Mom, where did the great abandonment cycle begin? My birth mom abandoned me. You and Daddy Number One adopted me. Saved me, actually. But then handsome, wonderful Dad left us when I was three and a half. Abandoned by Dad. Saved by you, Mom. That's when we really became "Us." Dad left "Us" for another woman, who was a great cook and seamstress, and wouldn't you just know it, she was even a nurse. She was like Fertile Myrtle, and in no time flat they had four "real" biological boys, not the secondhand recycled kind of kid like me. When my much younger, sexier stepmother had those four real boys, we became even more "Us."

Never being a conventional mom, you adopted a whole new group of friends: gay men. Of course, I was too young to know what that meant. I thought they were just very creative, and dressed well. I called them "uncles." And then we married one.

Life was glamorous and grand in Honolulu and smelled perpetually of heavenly tropical aromas. I loved Hawaii.

I loved my hula lessons. Shaking my tiny hips to "Little Brown Gal," my extra-special number, never failed to bring down the house.

I was so fortunate, I even went to a private school, Punaho (Obama's school) which I I loved especially since I got to go barefooted. Bake (my stepfather) and I, with hot pink hibiscus flowers behind our ears, would pick fresh papayas from the tree in our backyard. We'd bake them and add just a squeeze of lemon and a shake of nutmeg so they tasted amazing, like exotic sweet potatoes.

Two years later, when Bake's gig in the Army was up, we moved to his hometown, Huntington, West Virginia, where people cut grass instead of wearing grass skirts. Compared to Hawaii, I didn't like it much. I shouldn't refer to the kids there as hillbillies, but let's just say they actually did find packing a peanut butter and jelly sandwich lunch and climbing hills fun. I didn't. I preferred gardenias and papayas.

Then my "very creative" stepfather got a snappy new job with Stouffer's Foods in Chicago. We moved there with him to the downtown area, where the "El Train" seemed to rattle above our heads in our small apartment. I had never lived in such a big city. It was kind of scary. Not only was Chicago windy, but the kids in my new inner-city school came in more colors than M&M's and were very unfriendly to me. I was used to being liked. Being totally out of my element, I was fairly terrified going to school each day.

Night after night, Bake would stay out later and later. Then one night he didn't come home at all. Mom's previous two husbands (she'd been married once before adopting me) had left her for another woman. I'm pretty certain she wanted to make sure that never happened again. And it didn't. Bake left "Us" for another man.

But before he could officially jilt "Us," Mom shook me one gray morning at five o'clock in my newly acquired time zone and said, "Let's get out of here right now, okay, honey?"

I was half asleep, half confused, and half frightened but one hundred percent happy about leaving this big, scary, unfriendly city.

Now, what exactly was her plan this time? To be honest, I didn't really care. I was so happy just to be getting out of Dodge. And I was so delighted not to have to spend another frightening day in that gigantic school with strange kids who hated me.

I said, "Fine, Mom" and packed, completely shaking in a jumbled jiffy.

Basically abandoned by Bake, we were very clever and abandoned him first. We sort of stole our own car. It was the one Mom and Bake owned jointly. It was the one he would never see again. In fact, he would never see me or the Chevy again.

And the abandonment cycle continued. We were on the road again. You saved me again, Mom. It was once again "Us" against the world in our two-tone blue Chevy on Route 65 driving to Cincinnati, where people were normal. We were going to Aunt Alice's home, who was to take us in while we licked our relationship wounds. And then we would go into our Daddy rehab with only two very exclusive members: you and me, Mom.

On the drive, Mommy dearest, you were probably so upset at yet another failure that we argued. As the car accelerated, our arguing accelerated. As the car radio got louder, our screaming got louder. We were probably yelling about something stupid."Mom. I'm hungry; can we stop for lunch? I want a cheeseburger and french fries with a Cherry Coke.""No, Gayle, not yet. I want to go another twenty miles before we stop."

"Twenty miles? No! I'm hungry now! I want a cheeseburger now!"

A cheeseburger, of course, was not the issue. The point was "We" had failed once again to hold onto our man. Our arguing escalated as our all-too-familiar flight-or-fight mode was once again happening and crazily merging into our clashing wills. Our mutual hurt, guilt, and rage were spiraling out of control.

You screamed at me, "Gayle, get out of the car."

You stopped the car on Route 65. You opened the door and shoved me out on Route 65. Now I was totally alone, abandoned by the only rock I knew, even if my rock was a rolling stone. I was in more terror than I had ever been in my life, because I just got abandoned by "Us."

I was standing all alone on a chilly September morning on Route 65 in the middle of nowhere with cars zooming by wondering what was to become of me. Then my heart suddenly did leap up. You did a U-turn. You were coming back. The two-tone blue Chevy was coming toward me. You flung the door open to invite me back into our cycle I rushed back into the warmth of familiarity. Always abandoned. Always saved by "Us." By you. By me. By me. By me.

*Alex Gleckler, Daddy #1.*

*Burt Dusterberg, Daddy #3.*

*After not seeing my Daddy #1 for ten years, visited Hartford, CT., and met my four half brothers. In this picture. From left to right: Jim, Tom, Bill and Bob Gleckler.*

# *First Daddy, Second Chance*

### Age 17

I drove up in our '55 two-tone green Chevy onto the driveway of our humble red brick home in Mariemont, a suburb of Cincinnati. As a junior in high school, I had grown to my full height of five foot six and had "filled out" about as much as I was going to fill out, which was nothing to write home about. I was extremely tan, wearing white short shorts, with a tight turquoise T-shirt to match my eyes. My zits, thank God, had at last vanished, so I was pretty much a finished teenage product. As I approached our screened-in front porch, I heard my mom and my stepfather talking. My stepfather Burt was my Daddy Number Three whom mom married when I was thirteen. Then I heard a third voice, a voice that I swear resonated in my very soul. It was from some faraway three-year-old child hearing place, unfamiliar yet familiar, in some spooky way. With trepidation, I slowly opened the squeaky screen door. Then I saw HIM.

My mother said, "Gayle, say hello to your father."

My who? Oh no, you must be kidding me! My stranger-than-fiction daddy who deserted me ten years ago? How can she spring this on me? And my stepfather, Burt, was sitting in his Lazy Boy lounge chair, in as much shock as I was. Surprises can be great. This was more like the surprise from hell.

I stuck my more than a child but not yet a woman, seventeen-year-old hand out to meet his. No one ever explained to me what the proper etiquette is when you meet the father who ditched you ten years ago. This spontaneous unwanted reunion was beyond awkward. I basically just wanted to put this horror film into reverse and jump back into the two-tone Chevy, drive away, and never speak to any of them again.

But I was too well behaved to do such a rebellious thing. Poor Burt, who was a shy introvert in comfortable situations, was beside himself. His Germanic, tight, thin mouth had withdrawn so far in, his lips seemed to have disappeared.

"Sit down and join us, Gayle," said Mom, pretending to be nonchalant.

I kept crossing and uncrossing my legs nervously. On some level I wanted to punish him and make him feel guilty for ditching an innocent little girl who had by now almost grown into a teen babe. The possibility that I would ever see him again in my life had never even occurred to me. I certainly never banked on it. The only thing I could bank on with my father was the predictable $25 checks that came like payoff clockwork on my birthdays and Christmas, adding up to $50 a year. His love was cheap. My inner seductive child knew I could still win him back if I really wanted to.

Breaking rudely into my revengeful fantasies, Mom said, "Gayle, go change your clothes because your father wants to take you out to dinner."

Out to dinner? Was she kidding?

Didn't she always tell me not to get into a car with a stranger? Now she' was sending me away with one. I hated her for putting me in this position. I went upstairs in a daze to the safety of my girly bedroom. All I could focus on was the eternal teenage question: "What in the world should I wear?"

Should I dress pretty so he decides to "keep me" this decade or ugly so he knows he made the right decision to dump me? Or I could go with a medium cute look to hope for a raise to $100 a year. I chose the obvious. I went for pretty, determined to make him eat his heart out for abandoning me.

When uncomfortable, my mom mysteriously acquired an upper-class English accent. She had affected a very convincing one now: "Well now, yooou twooo have a loooovvvveerly dinner."

Burt's defeated features had now given way to a look of resistant resignation. "Have a nice time," he muttered reluctantly.

Poor Burt. Poor Gayle. And as we pulled away I realized, Poor Mom. Her worst nightmare had just arrived unannounced from Hartford, Connecticut. Who the hell did this guy think he was arriving on our doorstep after ten years? I faked a goodbye smile. Mom and Burt did too. Then off I went in the car with the stranger, who didn't even have the decency to lure me in with chocolate.

As we were driving into downtown Cincinnati, I noticed he was very odd. He had a gravelly voice with a very unique accent. I later learned why. It was actually a strange blend of his birthplace, Berlin, Germany, and Hell's Kitchen, New York, where he and his parents had settled after they immigrated. It was then folded into a Bronx accent, followed by Columbus, Ohio, and now Hartford. What a cacophony of sounds, like some strange Daddy jazz. I noticed as he was driving that his hands shook with a slight but constant tremor. This twitch thing scared me more than his peculiar way of speaking. We were an accident waiting to happen as we attempted awkward introductory conversation. How does one make casual talk with a father you haven't seen in a decade?

"Gayle, do you like sports?"

"Not too much, except for volleyball. And you, are you into sports?"

"Well, I like to fish, and I love baseball, especially the Cleveland Indians. Remember when you were little and we would listen to the games on the radio?" Actually, I did, but I said no. At the best Italian restaurant in Cincinnati we stumbled through dinner, trying to fill in a ten-year gap. By dessert my faux dad had in some way charmed me, being handsome, warm, and funny. Funny always gets me. It's my Achilles' love button.

Even if I set out to hate him, I found myself warming up to him. When the purpose of his surprise visit became clear, I was somewhat open to his proposal. He wanted to right a wrong, to get to know me, and for me to know him. The only way to do that meant going to Hartford to meet my stepmother and four half brothers, Bob, Bill, Jim, and Tom.

As he drove me home, I was so conflicted. Even if I was curious enough to take him up on his offer, how could I discuss this with my mother? I was extremely afraid she would be very hurt at the thought of it.

The next morning I spoke to my mom, who had, thank heavens, lost her phony English accent and had come back to her Midwestern authentic senses. I told her what he had requested. She paused before answering me, then said graciously, "Gayle, I think it's a good idea for you to go this summer to get to know your father, stepmother, and brothers. You have a whole family you have never even met. You might really enjoy it."

One month later I flew on Eastern Airlines to Hartford. In a pathetic attempt to look like a gorgeous stewardess I wore my prom dress, an adorable white fluffy number, with white buttoned gloves and three-inch white leather pumps. I walked cautiously, descending the airline stairs in my virginal white splendor.

I gazed down at my decidedly handsome, tan, blue-eyed father. Yes, it was true, I was still very vulnerable when it came to him. If I dared to allow myself to love him, would he abandon me again? And there they were, my adorable half brothers all dressed up in suits with clip-on bow ties, standing in stair-step formation. At the bottom of the stairs they stuck out their chubby little hands and, obviously well rehearsed, said, "Hello, sister. Hello, sister. Hello, sister. Hello, sister." I didn't know whether to laugh or cry, they were so precious.

My stepmother, June, smartly waited in the car in the parking lot until my father and brothers greeted me. I liked June almost immediately and almost as immediately felt guilty about betraying my mother.

June turned out to be one of my best friends ever, something I could never tell my mother. I could never tell her we drove around in June's white Cadillac convertible and pretended we were sisters. That summer I learned to adore my father all over again. It was like that delicious feeling you experience when you get an old boyfriend back, who realized he missed you so much he couldn't stand life without you.

And my brothers turned out to be very lovable. They taught me wonderful boy lessons, like it's not only okay to belch, fart, and tell really stupid jokes, it makes life a whole lot more fun. They, in fact, made my life a whole lot better.

When I returned to Cincinnati after this life-changing experience, it was too bad I couldn't tell my mother what a great time I had with so many new discoveries. I just couldn't hurt her. But now knowing how damned smart my mother was, I imagine she knew what a wonderful summer I had shared with my new family. And she even knew enough to know why I didn't tell her.

*Me as a Senior at Mariemont High School, Cincinnati, OH.*

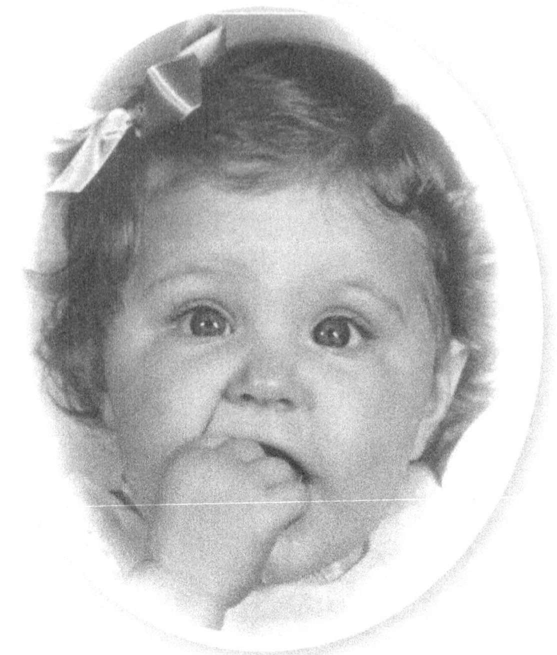

*Me at six months old.*

*Zac at six months old.*

# Whoops

Age 41

I never told Zac that when I was pregnant with him, his working name was Whoops. My boyfriend, Ken, and I moved in together because both of our leases were up in NYC. Always an excellent start—real estate desperation. We were lucky enough to get a massively sensational apartment in Tribeca overlooking the magnificent Hudson River. There was very little to do there, though, because Tribeca wasn't developed yet, so we did what we knew how to do best on frigid New York nights.

I was a total workaholic career girl with my own advertising agency, Gleckler & Spiegel. I was forty-one and Ken, forty-nine. I had over the last two years decided I wanted a child very much.

I myself am adopted, and I was told that if you adopted a child, you often wound up getting pregnant. I decided to sponsor a Haitian child by paying a monthly fee to Save the Children. When her precious photograph and simplistic profile arrived, I carried her picture with me everywhere. When I went to chic dinner parties in New York, I would whip out the photo and say, "Let me show you my new child." Of course, this was very glib and always attracted warm attention.

I guess even this faux adoption worked, because soon afterward I began noticing that something was definitely different about me and my body, but I couldn't put my finger on it. I asked Ken to have lunch with me in SoHo for a very special intimate discussion.

"Honey, I feel different. My body feels odd. My breasts are swollen. But at my age and your age, I couldn't possibly be pregnant." He nonchalantly said, "Oh, yes, you probably are. I am The Great Impregnator."

"You are The Great WHAT?"

He proceeded to tell me that he got his first girlfriend, Bunny from the Bronx, pregnant when she was only thirteen and he fourteen. Then Ken went on and on, almost boasting that he had many other unwanted pregnancies with girlfriends in his forty-nine years. Early in my relationship with Ken there were so many little questions that slipped my mind to ask, like, "By the way, are you 'The Great Impregnator' I've heard so much about?"

I took three drugstore pregnancy tests that all read positive, but I totally didn't trust them or believe them. I went to my Ob-gyn to take a real pregnancy test, and it was actually true. I was pregnant! I couldn't believe it. I was ecstatic, elated beyond my wildest dreams.

I had thought at my age, my eggs were certainly deviled by now, and at Ken's age, his swimmers must surely have been pickled. But there it was. We had, in fact, conceived Whoops, the geriatric love child I had always dreamed of and the one Ken had nightmares about. Ken could not conceive of having another child (he already had two almost grown daughters by his first marriage whom he loved dearly), but he definitely wanted me to get an abortion.

I said, "No way. I have always wanted a child."

We fought. We fought hard. We fought badly.

Finally, I said, "If I can't have this baby, I will commit suicide."

Now, I was not about to commit suicide, but he bought it. We then went to California to tell my mom, stepfather and his mom our extraordinary news.

But driving to my parents' condo in Coronado, California, I said, "You know, Ken, I'm from Ohio. I can't tell my parents I'm having a baby and not be married."

"Okay, let's get married." Another very romantic beginning.

"Hi, Mom. Hi, Burt. Guess what? Ken and I are getting married."

Mom said, "Oh, darling," and hugged me. Turning to Ken, she said, "We are so happy for you. That's just wonderful!"

"Oh, and by the way, we're having a baby." Talk about a pregnant pause. I thought they would both have heart attacks. No kidding. But after they recovered, they could not have been happier.

Anyway, my son, the joy of my life, I am so happy you exist. I am so thrilled that you are my dear love child. And your dad, whom you are the spitting image of, loved you unconditionally from the moment he held you. And he never stopped loving you every day of his life.

So, my dear Zac, I will never think of you as Whoops but as pure as love can be.

*Alex Gleckler, Daddy #1 staging a "Shotgun Wedding 'Ken better marry you'" in the Hamptons 1983.*

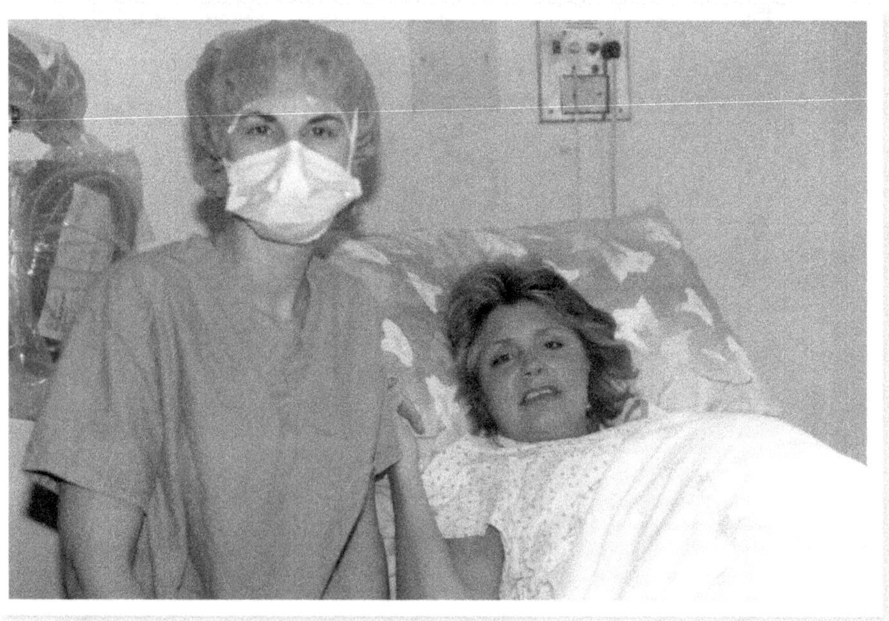

*Dr. Beth Lieberman, my surgeon and lifesaver, January 6, 1984.*

# The Verdict

## Age 41

Ken and I attended a Lamaze course when I was pregnant. This was to ensure that "we" would have a smooth natural childbirth. This was 1983, and being in our forties, we were by far the oldest couple in the class. The other soon-to-be first-time parents were all in their twenties. We looked like first-time grandparents.

The reason I fell in love with Ken was he was the funniest man I had ever met. To add to his outrageous humor, he was quite stylish: think Don Johnson in Miami Vice. Picture this: Ken wearing a peach-colored T-shirt under a beige linen jacket that hung just perfectly over his broad shoulders, pleated khaki pants, and soft, light brown loafers with no socks. I've always fallen for that look. A man wearing shoes without socks drives me crazy. It's like having wild, unprotected sex with his feet. He was cool. Beyond cool. He invented cool.

He often took me to the "in" place in Manhattan, Elaine's, where the owner and main draw, Elaine Kaufman, would greet him with her sharp signature wisecrack. This was her approving nod that Ken was in her inner circle. When we would stroll there, strutting our stuff on the Upper East Side on a sultry summer evening, every other person seemed to know him. In fact, I'm not absolutely sure, but I'm pretty certain I got pregnant just walking to Elaine's.

I was known as the class clown in high school, so it was no wonder that in our Lamaze class we instantly became known as the old funny ones. The nervous young couples came to count on us for comic relief. Of course, no mother-to-be could have been more anxious than I was, especially because by now my birth canal looked more like Guadalcanal after all it had seen in forty-one years.

After months of Lamaze, all of our bellies were getting bigger and bigger as it was about time for us to pop out babies. Then fewer couples showed up to our class every week because they either had a premature baby or chickened out entirely and decided to give birth the old-fashioned, drugged-up, painless way.

The instructor said, "Well, since we are down to the wire, let's have a couple come up and demonstrate the right way to breathe properly and give birth naturally." No one raised their hands, so the teacher called on the usual suspects. "Okay, Gayle and Ken, come on up and show everyone how to do it."

We obediently did as she asked. I lay down with my legs open and bent. Thespian like, I pretended to do real pushes, emulating all those birthin' baby scenes I'd seen in movies dozens of times. Ken, holding my hand, started counting in some vaguely similar way to how she had instructed us during these critical deadline weeks. Just by counting and making scary "I'm not sure I want to be a father" faces, Ken was already getting big belly laughs. Our teacher instructed me to go into heavier labor. I called on my failed improv acting class techniques and dug up some pretty impressive, convincing false labor moves. I greatly dramatized my faux contractions and moaned as if I were getting really uncomfortable. I imagined I was having real pain. I was so convincing, I actually started to believe it myself. I began to scream in earnest.

Ken, holding a stopwatch, was supposed to keep a calm, cool head and say, "Gayle, just remember to breathe while I count and time your contractions." I screamed again in mock pain, and Ken yelled out to our make-believe doctors and hospital staff, "Just give her the fuckin' drugs!"

The class cracked up. We failed miserably in Lamaze class but succeeded doing what we did best together, get the big yucks.

Zac was due on December 25, my own little baby Jesus. And, trust me, I knew I was being blessed with a miracle baby, especially since I was as far from a virgin as New York was from Bethlehem. I owned my own agency at the time, and worked right up to Christmas. I was decorating Zac's room, making collages and artwork for his unique baby boy nursery. Christmas came and went, but Zac did not come.

On New Year's Eve, Ken and I went to a fabulous party with all our best friends, who tried hard to rock and roll Zac out. We did everything short of breaking my water with an hors d'oeuvre toothpick, but he was having none of it. Zac must have been laughing at us, comfortably swimming around in lots of warm "hot tub Mommy water." So New Year's 1984 came and went with no appearance by our mystery fetus.

Over the next few days Ken and I saw every movie in town and ate at our favorite Tribeca neighborhood restaurant, The River Run, where we often saw Robert De Niro and Harvey Keitel, who ate there frequently.

"Zac, you better come out right now; you are missing real movie stars."

But celebrity spotting didn't seem to motivate him. In fact, nothing seemed to motivate him. During this extended waiting period, I was especially fixated on creating the perfect Lamaze bag, which I got at Bloomingdale's and filled with expectant goodies. This primo accessory was stuffed to the brim with all top-of-the-line things, including: adorable little pillows, wet wipes, Zac's first outfit, and multicolored, fruit-flavored candies for me to suck on while I was in labor.

Dr. Beth Lieberman, my wonderful, loving, but quite serious Ob-gyn, said, "Gayle, it doesn't look as if your son is going to be born naturally. We should schedule you for a C-section."

Was she nuts? After months of Lamaze classes and my over-the-top, most excellent Lamaze bag, a C-section? Oh no, not me! I couldn't believe my pregnant ears.

We scheduled our natural, unnatural happening to take place on January 6, Epiphany, a perfect day for my savior to be born.

I was clueless that January 5 was the full moon. Who knew that this lunar lunacy and shift causes women's water to break and that an abnormal number of women go into labor on that day?

On the night of January 5, 1984, water could be heard gushing from women's wombs all over Manhattan. And these mothers were all headed for NYU Hospital, including Ivana Trump, with her third child, Michael.

Ken and I naively got into a cab at 5:00 a.m. on January 6 and directed the cabbie to go to NYU Hospital, where I was scheduled to be the first in surgery around seven o'clock for my C-section. But guess what? Naturally, the full moon natural birth moms came first for the delivery room, so I was put at the end of the line. It was like I was taking a number at Zabar's. Cruelly, however, I wasn't allowed to eat lox and bagels. In fact, I couldn't eat anything.

We waited for hours. I was starving. Ken had an egg, sausage, and cheese sandwich. The staff took x-rays to see if Zac had dropped so they could induce my labor, but no such luck, Zac was still swimming around in my hot tub, I think somewhere near my tonsils. They couldn't induce. This boy had no intention of coming out on his own.

He was going to come into this world gently, not squishing painfully through a narrow passageway. He was making an entrance into this world slowly and easily, on Zac time.

So I waited. We waited. I was getting hungrier and hungrier, just famished.

Ken had a turkey and Swiss on rye with extra mayonnaise and mustard, but I couldn't eat a thing before having the epidural for the C-section. Ravenously, I started hitting my Lamaze bag stash. First I ate the red LifeSavers, always my favorites. When I ran out of reds, I had to resort to oranges. Next, I hit the yellows. As a last ditch, I started sucking up the greens. I was almost all out of colors when Dr. Beth came in about noon.

"Okay, Gayle, it's time for your epidural. Feeling okay?"

Feeling okay? Other than being fat as a pig, starving, nervous as hell, and next to my "Get the fuckin' drugs" husband? Oh sure, I felt just fine.

"Now, you haven't had anything to eat, have you?"

I said, "No. Well, nothing except the hard candies in my Lamaze bag."

"You had what? You know you can't eat before having anesthesia." She was furious with me and made no bones about it.

"Well, Beth, I consider a cheeseburger real food. I don't consider these LifeSavers food."

Dr. Beth adamantly felt differently. "Didn't you see the movie The Verdict?" she said.

Well, of course I had. Paul Newman, as a brilliantly drunk attorney, was the defense lawyer for a family whose daughter had become a vegetable because a surgeon neglected to tell her she couldn't eat before having anesthesia. She choked on her own vomit and went into a ten-year coma, never to wake up.

Okay, this was swell. To compound my anxiety, this woman who was about to cut me open and go in to fetch the most beautiful thing that ever happened to me was totally pissed at me. Great. Just great. She did, however, okay the anesthesiologist to give me the epidural around 12:30 that might turn me into a vegetable.

An hour later I was rolled me into the delivery room right after Ivana Trump. How could a vegetable raise a beautiful baby boy, I thought as I lay there. And Ken, who had begged me to get an abortion because he was too old to start a new family, would now have to raise Zac as a single parent. The LifeSavers were not stopping Dr. Beth from taking a chance on mine.

The nurses covered me from the waist down so I couldn't see a thing, but, unfortunately, I could hear everything.

"Okay. Hand me the scalpel," Dr. Beth said, just like in the movies. Here I was, the star of my own movie, and I had just eaten the killer props.

Cut. Cut. I could hear Dr. Beth and the nurses talking. I could hear everything but felt nothing because I was completely numb.. However, I was way too mentally keen from the waist up. I felt as if I were in a horror movie and having an out-of-body experience. Not at all numb to their conversation, I heard them talking about someone, and that someone was me. I couldn't believe I could hear the very angry Dr. Beth actually say, "What tight muscles you have, Gayle! What a shame I have to cut them."

I was thinking, Thanks for telling me that. Just cut away my previously flat belly, and thanks for the warning announcing my fat-bellied future. But who cared? It was all for Zac.

"Oh, Gayle! He's perfect. Gayle, he's beautiful!" Zac cried on cue after Dr. Beth slapped his back, just like in all those newborn scenes I'd seen in the movies. Dr. Beth held Zac up. All toes and fingers were accounted for. Then she weighed and measured him. "Gayle, he's nine pounds, eight ounces, and twenty-one inches long. Just perfect."

Then the nurses swaddled my savior in the standard soft baby blue-and-pink-striped blanket. They showed him to me. He and his blanket didn't look at all standard to me. He was in fact a miracle, my miracle. In four days I would be forty-two, and he would be four days old. God had been unbelievably good to me. I was ecstatic. Zac was alive, well, and beautiful. And I wasn't a vegetable.

"Wait a minute," I heard Dr. Beth say. "What's this? And what's that?" Dr. Beth and her fastidious attendants were peering up close and personal inside me.

The green draping obscured my view, as well as any possible understanding of what was going on inside of me. It was beyond bizarre.

"Gayle, I see something I don't like." "Like what? A bad twin?"

"You have polyps in your abdomen; in fact, quite a few." Dr. Beth's bedside baby manner left a bit to be desired.

"Gayle, I want a second opinion," she said. "I am calling in another surgeon. Give Zac to his father."

I'm once again panicked at the thought of Ken being a single parent to the child he never wanted.

In walked a very handsome doctor (like an ER George Clooney), dressed in light green accessorized perfectly with plastic gloves to match. He had a well-scrubbed confidence about him. Never more vulnerable in my life, and just freshly fillet, I saw all these heads disappearing under my intimate green tent to confer.

The handsome surgeon emerged from my insides and said, "Yes, I think you should remove all the polyps, Beth."

All the polyps? Who am I, an ecstatic new mom exploding with cancer? "Gayle, I think these polyps should all be taken out, so we can biopsy them."

"Beth, you are already in there," I remember saying. "Just take out any foreign objects you don't like, old skate keys, Coke cans... "

Dr. Beth said to the anesthesiologist, "Please give her another epidural because this surgery is going to take at least another hour."

Oh, swell. If the red LifeSavers hadn't killed my brain cells yet, we had another hour of anesthesia to move swiftly into the orange, yellow, and, dear God, please, let's not get into the greens. I was having schizoid thoughts. The most wonderful thing that had ever happened to me had now plunged me into sheer terror.

I had a beautiful baby boy and possibly cancer.

But a very sweet thing happened. Ken, Mr. "Get an abortion; get the fuckin' drugs," had the first three hours bonding with his only son, who at the moment of birth looked exactly like him. Zac was his clone.

After three hours, I woke up from my nightmare in a dream state.

In a day or two the biopsied polyps were found to be benign, but in fact, Beth was right on. They were precancerous. I was breast feeding my gorgeous miracle child and thinking, I am doubly blessed.

I gave Zac life, and he saved mine.

*Ken Weiner, Zac and me when we were happy.*

*Zac at three, a perfect height.*

# Measured In Inches

Age 12-60

I am never really separated from my mother—now or ever.

I am never really separated from my son—now or ever.

But if I were to describe the relationships between a mother and daughter and a mother and son, as preposterous as it sounds, I can measure them fairly well in inches. As best as I can, I will take out my emotional tape measure to illustrate this concept for you.

**Mom's Inches**

It all had to do with height. My mother was five foot nine and always wore three-inch heels, making her six feet tall. Being so tall, especially considering when she was born, in 1903, was extremely rare. I had little choice. I had to look up to her.

When she described the man I should marry, she would always start with "Gayle, look for a tall, smart, polite man. And don't forget, it's just as easy to marry a rich man as a poor man."

I think just to spite her, I first married a man who was only five seven.

My next husband was only five foot six. My third was a towering five ten. The smart and polite part was definitely in place. But tall and rich? Most certainly not!

As a child, my mom was a giant in my eyes. She was a dynamic, articulate woman who was extremely intelligent and popular, a deadly combination. In an argument no one could ever win against her charismatic, towering power, especially short me.

As my body started to grow, so did my wisecracking mouth. I actually dared to talk back to my mommy giant when no one else would chance it. But I was also growing in stature. At five foot six in sixth grade, I was the second tallest girl in the class.

When I was a teenager and got dressed up, I wore three-inch heels. Wearing them, I grew to an imagined womanly five nine. You see, I had height confused with maturity. My new high-heeled self was not exactly standing eye to eye with Mom, but I was closing in, or, should I say, up. The playing field was leveling. As she got older, Mom started wearing lower heeled shoes and also began to shrink.

I moved to Manhattan in the late '60's after college and started working my way up the ad game ladder during the Mad Men days. Mom had retired and was shrinking more daily. She was hardly the towering giant she once was. The high heel was now on the other foot.

In fact, she was diminishing in almost every way, becoming a nice older woman who looked and sounded like most women her age. She softened. As Mom lost her edge, I grew mine. We were at last beginning to even out in height and separate emotionally. Of course, as much as I fought her towering power over me when I was younger, I now felt sad and actually missed it.

**Zac's Inches**

I was almost forty-two when Zac was born, unheard of in 1984. And now look. I was blessed with the perfect twenty-one-inch-long Zachary. I thought I had died and gone to heaven. Mercifully, Ken was five feet, ten inches tall, so Zac had a fighting chance at height.

As life went on, my five ten husband was also shrinking in my eyes daily in a fairly loveless marriage. I lost him to a hot-and-heavy affair he was having with Absolut Vodka. We discovered in first grade that Zac was dyslexic. Ken and I separated. I moved to Millbrook, New York, where we lived in a renovated barn near the Kildonan School for Dyslexics.

I was now officially a single mother and worked as an advertising consultant at home, no easy task in the middle of nowhere. In the country and without Ken, Zac and I were now totally inseparable. I breakfasted him, dinnered him, homeworked him, tucked him in, and Good Night Mooned him every night, usually falling asleep cuddled up next to him. Waking an hour later, I silently crept out of his bed, turned off the lights, and thanked God for the great privilege of allowing me to be Zac's mother.

Those were delicious days, months, and years that melted together, wrapped in an intimate love of respect and mutual dependency during those precious elementary school times. We were the Two Musketeers. Zac was my best friend and I his. And I was so much taller, he had no choice. He had to look up to me.

Six years later we moved to Westport, Connecticut, and he was beginning to gain on me. I was still five foot six, and he was now five two. He started shooting up. He was getting bigger by the day, and so was his sassy mouth. Predictably on the dot of turning thirteen, he became my wise-ass teenager. What happened to my beautiful baby? Body hair began sprouting all over him. Then one day the telltale moment came (every mother of a boy knows this), I was never allowed to see him naked again.

I was proud that he was entering manhood, but I felt a certain loss of my baby and our special bonding. The Freudian separation was definitely happening right on schedule. When he was five three, then five four, then five five, I still had some semblance of parental authority. But one day, and I will never forget it, we were standing in the kitchen eye to eye. It was a face-off of wills and power. He was now five six.

The future was clear to me: I was about to go downhill quickly.

*Zac and me totally compatible in height and everything.*

As Zac grew to five-seven, five-eight, and five-nine, our arguments and power struggles grew louder. When he hit five-ten, he was now towering over me. He also actually began to look down on his infrequently visiting dad. His father rarely came over, but when he did, it was obvious to me he had now shrunk to five nine. And there it was: Zac had gained on both of us. Zac got his height. I lost my power. He was now looking down on me, probably in many ways.

Growth takes time. The emotional inches measured in those high school years were at times quite painful. But inch by inch we fumbled our way through his terrible teens. Now Zac is in his twenties, and when I see him across a room, my heart still leaps, and I think, who's that tall, handsome guy? Oh my God, it's my Zac!

Now he's mellowed and matured. When he comes up and gives me a hug, I am stunned at his manhood and height. Zac is now six feet tall, and he made it to my mother's description of the perfect man for me. He is tall, smart, and polite.

Rich? Well, that remains to be seen. But he and I are rich in the way that can only be measured: in love, not inches.

*Zac at 17, 3" taller than me. Power totally shifted.*

# Ten Stories by Eileen Grace

Taking Care

School

Cotton the Cat

Doing the Dishes

I Can't Look

The Punishment

Mom's Rocker

A String Of Beads

The Accident

A Letter To Mom

*My mom, Clarissa Murphy.*

# Taking Care

It had to do with the accident and the scarlet fever. As is so often true, I have a hard time imagining how my mother managed the challenges of her single-parent life.

When I was eighteen months old, I fell on the iron floor grate in the front hall of the one hundred-year-old  house where I grew up. The house back then was heated with coal, and the black, grid patterned grate was hot enough to grill steak. My thirteen-year-old brother Charlie peeled me off, and away we went to the hospital.

I got scarlet fever while I was in the hospital being treated for burns and had to stay for two months. The nuns told my mother not to come into the ward, but just to look through the door when she came to visit.

"She gets too upset when you have to leave," they said.

Penicillin was brand new back then. My mom was told she'd have to give me injections when I got home. Injections every four hours, even injections at two o'clock in the morning.

"Practice on a grapefruit," the nuns told her. Have you ever known a toddler to stay as still as a grapefruit? I still remember the black plastic box that held the needles.

Uncle Jack lived with us; he was my father's great-uncle. My father wasn't around; Uncle Jack was. The story was that he'd hold my head under one arm and my feet under the other when it was penicillin time. Headlocks aside, I was crazy about Uncle Jack and followed him around like a puppy.

All through my childhood, if I ever got a sore throat or an earache, my mom would treat it like typhoid fever. I stayed home from school, tucked into bed with tea and toast on a tray, listening to Arthur Godfrey on the radio. I can still hear her footsteps on the stairs, coming up with the tray. This advanced nursing talent was layered between her full-time job of getting out the U.S. mail. Fortunately, the post office was not far from home, and she'd run back and forth from work, a Postmistress acting like a bird flitting to a nest full of hatchlings. She was the best nurse-mother ever.

*Me and my brother Peter on right, with the Boy Scouts.*

# School

Infant Jesus Elementary School: I knew where it was; my brother went there. I also knew with a crushing feeling of dread that I didn't want to join him. I had just turned five, and the nuns at the school told my mom I was too young to enter the first grade. She was working full time, supporting the family and paying a baby sitter. She was not about to be intimidated by women in gray-and-white habits with huge rosaries hanging from their belts that rattled against their starched aprons.

Sister Gertrude, the principal, relented and said I could start that September. It was 1949, and I thought Sister Gertrude was the ugliest woman I'd ever seen.

There were forty kids in the first grade, all of them sitting primly at little wooden desks in a room with green walls. I learned to stand in line, to be quiet, to pay attention (kind of), and to recite my letters. Numbers were a different story. Shame is a feeling I still associate with most academic endeavors. There was a test in arithmetic as it was called back then. I had no idea how to count to one hundred.

The big windows in the classroom saved me. I was always looking out of them, wishing I was at the beach, in the marsh, at home, or at least the hell away from there. "A daydreamer," they called me, a daydreamer whose favorite time of day was three o'clock.

The other names weren't so nice: Fatso, Fatty, Tons of Fun, and, of course, the song "Fatty, Fatty two by four, couldn't get through the bathroom door, so she did it on the floor." These came from other kids in dark green uniforms with white blouses, kids who needed small and medium sizes instead of large. I began building a shell to hold the tears, to wear no expression.

When spring came and the nuns would select a little girl to wear a miniature habit and be the star of the May procession to the church, you can bet they never picked me.

I never belonged to the "in" group. My friends were outsiders just like me , but they made the school days somewhat bearable. I watched other kids get in trouble; I was too quiet to be noticed.

*My father, Edward Murphy, on left with geese.*

# Cotton the Cat

He shot my cat. My brother shot my cat. In a recent conversation he remembered that, yes, the cat was eating a bird, a wild canary or a Baltimore oriole, or maybe a redwing blackbird. There were so many birds in the marsh behind the house. Peter was very fond of birds.

"At the last minute, I moved the rifle and missed the cat, just scared it," he insisted. We did have a hunting tradition in our family. There were guns hanging above the fireplace and photos of black ducks held upside down next to men wearing high rubber boots and jackets with big pockets. My father built a duck boat. It rested in the marsh grass behind the house. It was a little like a canoe crossed with a kayak, and a wonderful color khaki green.

Never mind what Peter remembered; I never saw that cat again, and my mom was really pissed. She had a temper equal to Peter's. Thank God there was someone to stand up to him.

"Jesus, Mary, and Joseph! What have you done?! Put that gun away. You shot it? I can't believe you'd do something so horrible. You have no right to shoot her cat. Who do you think you are, some Irish vigilante? Don't talk to me about the bird. Remember, I'm the boss of this house, not you. Go clean up that mess and don't let her see. May God forgive you 'cause right now I can't." She turned away, flinging her hand above her forehead. "Get out of my sight!" she exclaimed and marched down the hall.

Mom wouldn't let me see the cat, a bloody mess it must have been, and she held me while I cried. She probably made him apologize, but I don't remember that part.

Peter disappeared for a while after that. He'd built a fort in the woods up the hill and spent some time there, waiting for Mom to cool off. Dinner was at six; he was home by then.

Cotton was white and looked good against the green grass all around. She was easy to spot on the unmanicured lawn. We had a dog, the family dog, but Cotton was my cat. Years later I got another white cat, maybe a descendant of the first.

Luckily, my brother lives in a town far away.

*In ascending order singing Murphy songs: Eileen, Peter, Ted, Charlie and Ann.*

# Doing the Dishes

My mother's kitchen was warm when the oven dial read 350 degrees. There was a red linoleum floor. Drafts came under the back door leading to the porch, and through the window cracks. Lots of life happened in that kitchen, and when the oven was on, even the wind off the harbor couldn't make us cold.

Mom was the Postmistress of the Mount Sinai post office. Mount Sinai, Long Island, was such a small town back then that the post office had to share a building with the general store. There was a wall of brass mailboxes, with a little window and brass turning knob on each box. The floor was wide boards worn rough from the heavy canvas bags dragged across them.

She knew everyone in town and would greet each person when they passed the counter window to go to their box and check for mail. They called her Chubby,  a nickname she'd had since school days and so familiar it was no longer an insult but simply a name. Her voluptuous body never conformed to her fantasy of being flapper slender with straight hanging clothes. Mom worked until six every night, came home to make us dinner, then went back to work to sort mail for the next morning. Sometimes she didn't get home again until eight or nine.

My brothers were in charge of doing the dishes after dinner. Charlie, the oldest, would pluck straws from the kitchen broom, hold them in his hand so just the tops showed, and instruct everyone to draw a straw to see who would wash. The short straw lost. That person would be the one to stand at the sink.

On the other side of the sink was the pantry. It had a door with a window, and inside were shelves for cups and saucers, plates and bowls. With the pantry at one end and the sink at the other; wash, dry, and toss was the routine. Dishes flew from hand to hand and made it safely to the shelves. I don't remember any landing on the red floor. Although there were no dishes crashing, the dish-washing process was far from quiet.

"Let's have a song," someone would yell, and then it would begin. We called them the Murphy songs, learned so early from Mom that it seemed we'd always known them.

"It ain't gonna rain no more, no more," Teddy would sing and beat out a rhythm with the nearest wooden spoon. I especially liked playing the pancake turner flipped upside down on the edge of the table. If I pushed down the handle, it would vibrate impressively and add nicely to the general chaos. Later, Peter learned to play the ukulele, and then we really sounded good.

After the dishes were done, there was homework to do, shoes to shine, and me, the youngest, to get ready for bed. Sometimes, if there was enough time before Mom was due home from the post office, we'd have the all-time best recreational activity: the washcloth fight.

This involved turning out every light, arming ourselves with sopping wet washcloths, and prowling through the dark house in a combo of hide-and-seek and dripping wet war game. I remember the huge wet spots on the stairway's striped wallpaper.

One of the reasons I so loved my mother was that when she did get home, she didn't seem to mind.

*Old white house, Mount. Sinai, Long Island, NewY.ork*

# I Can't Look

The old white house near the harbor had three floors. In the attic, wooden pegs held the roof beams together, and from the window you could see all the way to Connecticut. Worn wooden stairs led up to the attic, and that's where the summer clothes and Christmas decorations lived in the off-season. Sometimes when we had lots of company, I'd get to sleep up there and smell the special attic smell. I'd wonder if there wasn't some treasure I'd missed in the big trunks with their curved tops.

Mom was often rearranging things in the attic. In one half of it she fixed up a sleeping place for me, with a bed, a chest of drawers, and a really cute dressing table with a red-and-white-striped skirt. I loved to sit by the window, look down on the world outside, and see the branches of the big maple trees wave in the wind.

I was, and still am, very fond of trees. Even today when I meet an especially beautiful tree, I just have to give it a hug. That's how it was back then, but it wasn't just hugging, it was climbing too.

My specialty as an eight-year-old was disappearing.

The youngest of five, I could easily slip away from the general chaos of the household and not be missed. Dishes to do? I'd be gone. Woodpile to move? Time to go for a walk through the marsh, where the tall reeds hid everything. But the best hiding place of all was up in a tree.

Most people never looked up, and I would quietly sit on a high branch while they walked under me unaware. Mom was tolerant of my tree-climbing habits, as she was of my baseball, football, and basketball endeavors. She encouraged my tomboy status. "Go outside and play" was a familiar command.

One day my mom was working in the attic. I told her I was going outside. There was a very tall maple tree near the corner of the house, a friendly maple, with smooth gray-green bark and low branches inviting me up. A small boulder stood next to the trunk like a step to a front door. The first pull-up was the hardest, sometimes I had to hook a leg over a branch and hang upside down for a minute. Then it was like climbing a spiral ladder. It took me up and up. The green leaves covered me like a cloak. Soon I was at the top where the trunk thinned out and the branches showed some sky. If I leaned one way and then the other, I could make the tree sway a little, even though there was no wind. That's when I saw Mom in the attic window.

"Hey Mom!" I called. The window was open, so she heard me, but it took her a moment to realize I was right outside the window. I can't remember what she said first, maybe a moan or a groan or a very loud nonverbal exclamation. But I do remember the second part: "I can't look!" she cried and, covering her eyes, turned away from the window.

I'm reminded now of what she said that day. My third child, Jason, now a young man of thirty-two, recently left on a one-year walkabout, traveling to parts of the world Columbus never heard of. Jungles and deserts and beaches with mega surfer waves, earthquakes and civil unrest, all the adventures and unknowns I can't control make me cover my eyes and repeat my mothers words, "I can't look!"

*Me and my brother Peter Murphy.*

# The Punishment

They called the police. I was missing. It was January, the harbor was frozen, and it was dark out, after six o'clock. Six o'clock was dinner time and everyone was supposed to be home by dinner time.

Mother was frantic, eight-year-old girl missing, temperature twenty-nine degrees and falling. I did notice it was getting late but I was busy building an igloo with my friend, Tommy Butler. We used cardboard boxes to pack with snow and make blocks. His house, down along the harbor road, was one of the regular stops I made around town. Wandering was a favorite activity of mine.

I looked up from a perfectly formed white cube. "Uh oh, it's dark," I said and standing, brushed the snow off my mittens and headed home.

My boots crunched and squeaked on the barely plowed street. The snowplows seldom came around our neighborhood and when they did, gangs of hooligan snowball throwing kids would pelt the trucks and run. The windows of the old house glowed yellow through the dark. Warm light spilled on to the walk as I approached the front door.

I was greeted with relief, then with anger. "Where have you been?! How dare you worry us like this… you know the rules. Call the police; let them know she's back. I could brain you!"

Mother was really steamed; she was going for the hairbrush. She'd never hit me before. She'd hit my brothers but never me. She was going to do it though. What was it with hairbrushes anyway? The homecoming wasn't working out too well, it didn't look good.

Then he stepped in. He could have been a knight on a white horse, or even the cavalry come to save me from Indians circling the wagon train. The spanking seemed inevitable, she was that angry. But at the last minute, in the nick of time, my brother Peter stepped in and got between my mother and I. He blocked the hair brush and soothed her with reasonable excuses.

"She just lost track of time Mom, she didn't mean any harm. She's just a kid without a watch Mom, I'm sure it'll never happen again."

After a while it seemed safe to take off my snow pants.

*My mom Clarissa Murphy and her mother Anna Kern, circa 1908.*

# Mom's Rocker

She sat in her mother's lap, and wore a big satin bow in her hair. Her mother, my grandmother, wore a crisp high-collared Victorian blouse and skirt. Two-year-old Mom in a lace-trimmed dress was posing for the photographer. The photo is tattered at the edges, but the chair they sat in is oiled and proud and now resides in my kitchen corner.

They rocked in that chair, its mahogany arms and hand-carved back held them close. My brothers and sister rocked in that chair too, I remember, my feet barely touching the floor, gaining momentum, as I rocked on the wooden floor. That chair has been around forever, and if that chair could talk, we would have SOME stories.

My mother, born with a silver spoon in her mouth, pestered her father for another fur coat. She introduced her mother and father to the "peach of a guy" who would become my father: "Mother, Father, may I introduce Edward Murphy."

My controlling grandmother gave the bridal couple a cruise as a wedding gift, then completely decorated their new apartment while they were away. My sister Ann, the first baby, being rocked to sleep was oblivious of what was coming.

The 'peach of a guy', in drunken rage stormed around their apartment naked. That chair probably sustained its share of alcohol fueled abuse.

But today, when life is rough, I'm drawn to that chair, settle into its smooth wooden seat, feel its arms around me, feel all their arms around me, and just rock.

*My mom, Clarissa Murphy.*

# A String Of Beads

The dining room had over-the-top Victorian furniture. The feet on the pedestal table were carved lion's claws, and on the sideboard open mouths with fangs looked out over every meal. In the dark we'd hurry through that room, mirrors reflecting animals, foliage, tendrils, and teeth. At the age of four, hiding under the table, I liked to hook my fingers in the whittled out crevices on the table's feet.

That was where my mother said the rosary. She'd kneel in front of one of the chairs and lean her hands with the beads on the upholstered seat. "Hail Mary, full of grace, the Lord is with thee," she'd intone. The familiar words would echo through the downstairs rooms, and I would feel the familiar Catholic guilt because I didn't want to join her.

Mass on Sunday, no meat on Friday, venial sins, mortal sins, and always stand up when a priest enters the school room. Once I walked three miles to church on a Sunday morning after a heavy snow. The car was stuck. Nobody else in the family was going, but missing Mass was not an option for me.

After public high school, where I was known for NOT putting out, came Marywood, a Catholic women's college with Gregorian chant five times a week and rules, rules everywhere. Caps and gowns were required attire for Sunday Mass. Some girls wore them over pajamas and after service would go back to bed. In the cafeteria line, nuns would come around to measure the length of our skirts. All hail, modesty and invisible knees!

Hormones raging and frustration fuming, I barely made it to a white dress wedding right after graduation. In six months, I was pregnant and facing the legacy of my Irish Catholic mother with lots of babies. Mother had five, sister had six. Suddenly, birth control became an issue, and I began the painful process of leaving the faith. Adulthood overtook my beliefs and wore away a certainty about my religion. Questioning became norm, rebellion against the rules shook out the rigidity of my upbringing. God hadn't moved away; I had.

After years of saying no prayers, much less the rosary, a twelve-step program helped me understand the difference between religion and spirituality, and my concept of God swelled into something much bigger than a string of beads.

*My daughter and son Lisa and Christopher Grace in Florida.*

# The Accident

The sidewalk was next to a canal. Sunny Florida had water everywhere. The canal had wooden sides rising up four feet from the water's surface, with seaweed and barnacles showing where the deep tides rose and fell.

I held three-year-old Christopher by the hand, and my daughter Lisa walked behind, six years old and swinging her beach towel. Unbeknownst to us, an entire community of senior citizens watched our little parade from behind the windows of a nearby building.

Suddenly, there was a splash. Turning, I saw Lisa sputtering in the dark green water and the beach towel floating nearby. How deep was it? Alligators?

"Swim!" I yelled. "You know how to swim. Swim!" No "Oh, poor baby" from me, just the urgent command, "Swim!" And so she did.

Even though I was a lifeguard and swim teacher, with Lisa I'd never gotten past the dog paddle. The dog paddle worked. Keeping Christopher close, I flattened myself along the canal edge and stretching was just able to grab her reaching hand. A pull and a yank and scramble, and there she was, wet and scared but safe and breathing. I pulled her shivering little body close and stepped back onto the sidewalk. The beach towel sank out of sight.

That's when we realized that standing behind us were a dozen elderly Floridians with wide eyes, furrowed brows, and various expressions of extreme concern, each and every one offering to help. There probably was also a fleet of hungry alligators down the canal hoping for a variety of choices on the lunch menu: one tender young thing served over grandparent pasta.

Thanking our would-be rescuers politely, we moved on to drip dry, count our blessings, and firmly hold hands for the rest of the trip.

*From left: my son Christopher, me, my daughter Lisa, granddaughter Isabel, my son Jason and son-in-law Randy.*

*My grandaughter Isabel and my daughter Lisa.*

# A Letter To Mom

Dear Mom,

Thanks for helping me the other day. I think that was the only time since you've been gone that I called you that loudly. I still smile remembering the other time, on the beach that day. Me crying, "Where are you? You don't call, you don't write," and then looking up to see the horseshoe crabs, hundreds of them all along the water's edge. You taught us how special and ancient they are and how we needed to protect them. In so many ways you were ahead of your time.

Ann's son, Jimmy wanted her to scatter your ashes when we had your memorial service at Mount Sinai Harbor thirteen years ago. Since she was drunk and probably would have tipped the canoe, I did the ashes detail. Peter paddled in the stern and I sat in the bow with your special container. Didn't you love it that your ashes came through the mail? Did they know you were a Postmistress?

Ann stayed on the beach, she was the best sister, tipsy or not. I really thought I was prepared but when the moment came, it was a jolt to watch the water carry you away. Satterly's Landing is such a beautiful place, near the old house and the harbor.

Hope you approve of the site selection. Do you know when I visit there and think of you?

I think you do know, know it all, are it all. Wish I could talk over the Grover situation with you. My poor huband with advanced Parkinson's disease, is nursing home and wheel chair bound and breaking my heart in the journey to his end. You probably wouldn't tell me what to do, but I know what you would do.

We all recall the courageous way you nursed our father through his last days of colon cancer. How amazing your reunion was after all those years of married separation. I was so glad you had some fun at the end before he got sick. I heard you two did a mean Fox Trot.

Remember when I was newly married and living in Tarrytown? You used to complain that I didn't call you enough, said I didn't love you. That was always your best guilt manipulation, and I resented the pressure it put on me, resented the guilt.

Now it's my daughter, so busy with her life, who doesn't call me. Now I know how you felt and I wonder if someday Lisa will wish her daughter would call more often. It's all such a circle.

Let the water come and carry us away.

I love you,
Eileen.

# Eight Stories by Linda Howard Urbach

*It's 2:00 a.m. Do You Know Where ...?"*

*An Annoying Habit*

*Identifiable Markings*

*Learner's Permit*

*Little Mother*

*Mother-Daughter Outfits*

*The Birthday Card*

*The Invasion of Privacy Issue*

*Up to a certain age, I could always be sure where my little girl was.*

# "It's 2:00 a.m. Do You Know Where ...?"

Tucker picks me up at the station. I had taken the very last train from NYC, where I had gone to see the play, "Amy's View" with my friend Penny.

"What did Charlotte do tonight Tucker?"

"She went to Wilton with Joe and Chuck and Laura."

Who's Joe? Who's Chuck? I feel slightly panicky. And who does she know in Wilton? Wilton is a huge desolate forest dotted by multimillion-dollar houses that nobody seems to live in. Wilton makes Westport seem like a cozy neighborhood.

"She called to say she'd be a little late. There were cars blocking the driveway."

"What driveway? Whose cars?"

"She was home by twelve," Tucker quickly adds in an effort to calm me. "She was in a great mood, telling me about what a nice house Joe or Chuck had."

I'm thinking she came home late at night and had a conversation. With her father? As far as I was concerned, this was like an alarm going off.

Later that night, with Tucker snoring loudly, I go down to sleep on the living room couch. I hear Charlotte creep downstairs. A second alarm. She never gets up in the middle of the night, not even to go to the bathroom. I get up and go into the kitchen.

"What are you doing?" I practically demand.

"Drinking water."

Water? I know what water in the middle of the night means. Water means thirst, which means alcohol. Too much alcohol. I wasn't born yesterday.

"Why are you thirsty?" I ask in my best *Law and Order* voice.

Apparently, this didn't merit an answer. I ask again. She was drinking more water. "I don't know. I just am," she finally says.

The third alarm: she very rarely drinks just plain water. I have been standing in the kitchen for about two minutes before I finally come out with it. "Did you have anything to drink tonight?"

"You mean alcoholic?"

"Yes, alcoholic."

"No." That's it. Just a plain no.

I try to analyze what this no means. Is it no as in, No way: what do you take me for? No as in: Are you kidding? I wouldn't tell you anyway. No, as in: Don't be silly. I'm too young to drink? Or No as in: You caught me red-handed, and I have nothing further to say until my lawyer gets here.

She goes back to bed, but an hour later I hear her get up again. I find her standing in the dark in the kitchen. I think I see a car circling around the cul-de-sac.

"What are you doing up again?" I say.

"I'm getting something."

I don't ask what the something is. I get right to the point because nobody, no fifteen-year-old pip-squeak, is going to pull the wool over my eyes.

"Are you trying to sneak out?"

"What? No." Again, that plain, unadorned response.

"Who's out there? Is there some boy out there?"

She looks out the window. "There's nobody out there. What are you talking about?" "Amy's View", the play I had seen, is about a close but cantankerous mother–daughter relationship. At the end of the first act, Amy, the daughter, begs her mother not to say anything to the boyfriend about her being pregnant. Amy goes into a long explanation about how she has to handle this very carefully because she loves him and does not want to scare him away. The mother agrees not to say a word. She promises (cross-her-heart-and-hope-to-die) to let her daughter manage her own life because, after all, she is an adult. The boyfriend enters. The mother turns to him and says: "Amy has something to tell you."

The boyfriend is curious. The daughter is stunned.

We, the audience, gasp. How could she do this to her daughter? And then, while we are still sitting there breathless with disbelief, the mother hammers it home: "She's pregnant." It's a great curtain closer.

My conversation feels as if it comes right out of this play. How do I get Charlotte to talk, to open up to me without asking those questions that are guaranteed to close her curtain? What was she doing downstairs in the middle of the night? What is she doing hanging out with Joe and Chuck? Who are these boys? What do they do? What do they drink? Are there drugs? Is there sex? Will I ever really know what's going on in her life, in her head, in her heart? Not likely. All I can do is keep asking questions I never get answers for.

*Charlotte, never far from the beach.*

*Charlotte with her beloved uncles and her dear papa, (on right) at her Bat Mitzvah. Hebrew never became a habit.*

# An Annoying Habit

**The Smoker 1**

I can see it as clearly now as I did over forty years ago, the cigarette sitting in the ashtray burning, burning down and down, a thin stream of smoke rising into the air. The brands changed. First it was Camels, then Parliaments, then Merits or Vantage. But always there was a cigarette sitting in the ashtray or held between the first two fingers of her right hand, fingers that were short and plumpish but with long nails; long, strong nails, sometimes painted red, sometimes not, and always with the cuticles pushed back. "Never cut your cuticles. Always push them back," my mother said. I never understood the whole deal about cuticles in the first place. All I cared about was growing the nails. But I didn't inherit her strong nails. I did, however, inherit her love of cigarettes.

"I don't care if you smoke as long as you buy your own," she said.

"Never walk down the street smoking. It looks cheap."

"It's a filthy dirty habit," she would say as she lit up another. "I just hope you don't start." Too late. I had already started on Kent's, practicing in front of the bathroom mirror. I blew smoke rings, I inhaled, and, most glamorous of all, I French inhaled, which involved sucking the smoke up through my nose, down the back of my throat, and out my mouth. By the time I reached the ninth grade, I could perform a combo: French inhaling followed by a series of three perfect smoke rings. I held my cigarette with my first two fingers straight out like Katharine Hepburn. As years passed and I was now smoking in public and buying my own, I found that my mother's smoking annoyed the hell out of me. I began to chide her about it. "Do you have to smoke at the dinner table?" I said. "Your cigarette's burning," I would say. "If you're not going to smoke it, why don't you put it out?" I must have said this last one hundreds of times, barely concealing my annoyance.

To be honest, it wasn't so much the burning cigarette that annoyed me but her: her sweetness, her kindness, her passiveness, her shortness, her generosity, her patience, her unconditional lovingness, her eternal maternalness. In expressing my annoyance, I was letting out, in little dribbles, the anger I felt at her for just being my mother, and then, of course, the guilt that came with the anger that was camouflaged by the annoyance that seemed to be the theme of our mother–daughter show.

Back to the cigarette in the ashtray. She had an assortment of ashtrays, all of which I found equally annoying. She had the copper enamel ashtray that was part of her copper enamel collection, which was one of her many crafts. She had the ceramic shell ashtray, also another product of one of her hobbies/crafts. Most irritating of all was her collapsible portable ashtray that she had picked up at a garage sale. It folded in on itself and was no bigger than a pillbox. It even had a tiny ledge on which to rest a cigarette.

She would whip out the little sucker wherever smoking was permitted, which in those days was everywhere. I think this ashtray made her feel self-sufficient and independent, something that was always very important, given the fact that my father was the total boss of her world.

I have to say at this point that I was smoking as much as she was. I was smoking with more attention and energy. I never left a cigarette burning; no, I smoked it down to the filter. I smoked cigarettes so hard that invariably the burning embers would drop off the ends. I left burned holes everywhere, I mean everywhere: in my clothes, in other people's clothes, in rugs, on other people's expensive upholstered furniture. I left a track of burn holes over half the world.

But my burn holes were not the issue. It was my mother's smoking that was the problem. It was so annoying.

She had tried to downscale over the years from non filters to filters, from high nicotine to low, from tar to no tar. She was finally able to quit when she was diagnosed with lung cancer.

"It was easy," she said when asked how she had managed to do it. Also, it was easy to lose the twenty pounds she had tried to drop for years. She actually seemed happy that last year. The other shoe had dropped. She had always feared getting cancer, and now she had it. She didn't seem afraid of the dying part. She just wanted to make sure everything was in order. She was very busy in the end straightening drawers, throwing out old cereal, giving away her copper enamel materials.

She had happily stubbed out the last cigarette, washed out all the ashtrays, organized her dying and her death. When the small box that contained her ashes was buried, I thought again about her little portable ashtray—but no longer with annoyance.

**The Smoker 2**

Now it's years later. I am staring at some pictures taken of Charlotte and her friend Sarah from a recent trip to Costa Rica. Charlotte and Sarah are sitting at the resort bar that all the teenagers frequented every night. They are both holding fruity-looking drinks. Suddenly, I see a cigarette in my fifteen-year-old daughter's hand. At first I don't even react. For years every picture that was ever taken of me featured a cigarette. I don't think I have one photograph of me without a cigarette balanced between my index and third fingers. It was part of my body, part of my snapshot. And then I realize, this is my daughter, who doesn't even smoke.

This has been Charlotte's story about smoking: no, she doesn't smoke. She never smoked. She is not a smoker. When she would come home and occasionally smell of cigarettes, it was always from everyone else's smoking. When I smelled her breath, it was sweet and tobacco free. Now I think back and realize maybe it was too sweet. Maybe she brushed her teeth or took a breath mint. Now I have to confront her on this. I know she will have an explanation. She always does. What I don't know is whether it will be a lie or not. I never do.

Now, after having talked to Charlotte, I feel totally comforted. Her explanation of the picture with the cigarette:

"I was just posing. It was Sarah's cigarette."

"Sarah smokes?" Sarah is a big tennis player.

"No, not really." She points to the picture. "See? It's a full cigarette."

"But it's lit," I say.

"We don't smoke," she says. "Really."

And I believe her. Or, more precisely, I want to believe her. Then, apropos of nothing, she says: "I may want to major in early childhood development and teach elementary school." This is the first time she's even mentioned a major, a career—or college, for that matter.

I tell her she would be a wonderful teacher. And she would. Is this to throw me off the smoking trail? I don't know. But it works. It's as if she has taken me onto her lap, patted me on the back, and told me everything is going to be okay. Just as my mother would have done.

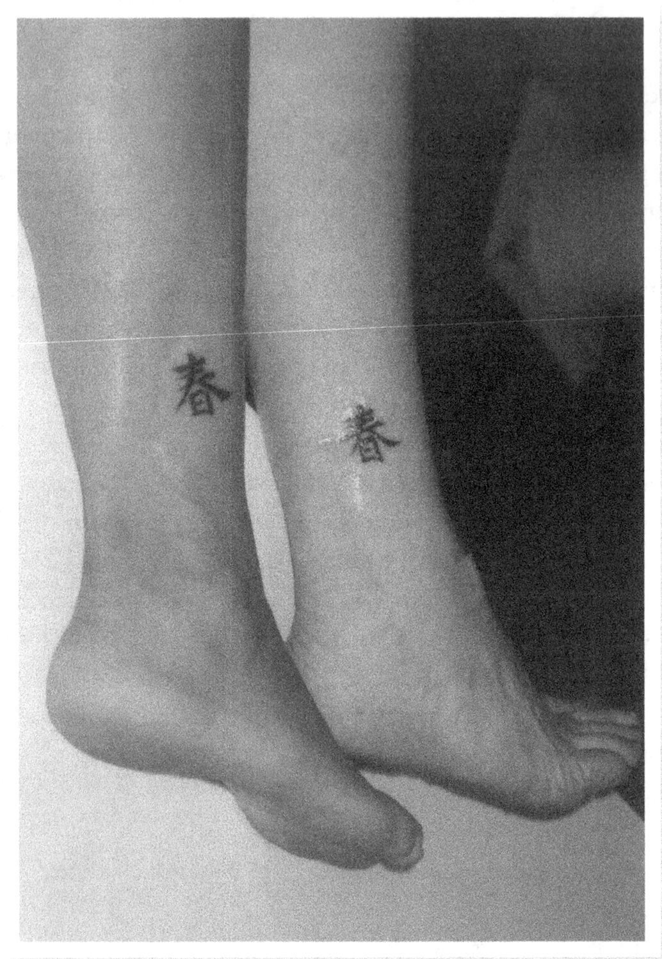

*Charlotte and my matching mother/daughter tattoos,
the Chinese symbol for spring.*

# Identifiable Markings

**Tattoos**

"I have something to tell you. Promise you won't be mad," my daughter Charlotte says.

I nod my head, enthralled with the idea that she actually wants to tell me something. She is bouncing up and down and on and off my bed. She acts like she is on speed or something. Is this what she wants to tell me, I wonder. Would she, in fact, tell me, having just taken the drug? Wouldn't she wait until she almost ODs?

And then I think: sex. And the next thing I think is: pregnant. Was that the something I had to promise not to get mad about? I am weighing all the possible options. I feel strangely detached. Herpes or petty larceny? Drug rehab? Abortion or adoption? Meanwhile, Charlotte is projecting all this energy. She seems very happy and very afraid to tell me at the same time.

"Promise you won't be mad. Pinkie-hope-to-die," she says, extending her little finger, which I clench in mine.

Suddenly, the answer comes to me like a psychic tweet: the tattoo is real!!! Days before I had noticed a design on her lower back.

"What's this?" I had asked, not for a minute thinking it was a real tattoo. It looked like a decal. Besides, tattoos were right up there on the No-No List with drugs, pregnancies, STDs, and shoplifting.

"Bunny did it with a pen," she said. And in order to appear cool in front of Bunny and Fifi, who were standing right there, I said, "It's a nice design, as long as it's not real."

Now, once the truth is out, she burbles forth with the whole story.

"I got the same one as Bunny and Julia. It was Julia's  idea." (Bunny and Julia are the evil sisters who live next door.) "We went to this tattoo parlor in Bridgeport." (Bridgeport!!!) "They had this design, but it was much more elaborate, so we redesigned it, and it was only $60, and it didn't hurt, it only tickled, and it was a very clean place, and the guy was very nice," she enthuses.

I am still with the tattoo is real!!!

I ask to see it again. I pay much more attention now that I know this is a mark that will forever deface the small of my daughter's beautiful back. The design is three intertwining soft-cornered triangles.

"What exactly does this symbolize?" I ask

"I think it's an Irish witch symbol, but I'm not sure."

"Be thankful at least that it wasn't a swastika," a friend comments later.

**Tongue Piercing**

"I'm sixteen years old. I can get my tongue pierced," says Charlotte.

This is now one year after the discovery of The Tattoo. I don't want to hear this. I am suddenly fed up with the nine holes in each of her ears, the naval piercing, the tattoo, all of it.

"Enough is enough," I say. "You can't do that. They could hit a nerve that will give you a permanent speech impediment. You can get an infection and have to have your tongue amputated. Or worse, you could chip a tooth. No. Absolutely not!"

She is as adamant as I am.

"I'm an adolescent. This is what adolescence is all about," she proclaims like some irate anthropologist. She is not about to skip one ridiculous teenage act. She is going for a perfect A in idiocy.

"You do this, and you can forget your ticket to California." (A very generous and now, I feel, undeserved birthday gift.)

"Fine. I'll buy my own ticket and stay there and never come back."

"Fine. And you can get someone in California to send you to college." I try to get control of myself to better explain my position. "Listen, I let you do this, and I let you do that, and instead of any of it satisfying you, you just want more. Now I am drawing the line," I say with a conviction that surprises even me.

She tries the reasonable approach: "The hole isn't permanent. It's not like a tattoo. I was going to get another tattoo on my ankle, but I thought, no, I'll get my tongue pierced instead." This is supposed to be a shining example of how levelheaded she is being. Then she runs through a list of friends, of people I've never heard of, who have their tongues pierced.

"I don't care!" I scream. It seems that these days I always end up screaming.

The good news: she comes back from the tattoo parlor without a hole in her tongue. They have told her that, in fact, she does have a vein running through the middle of her tongue and thus doesn't qualify for tongue piercing. We move on to a discussion of poking holes in your nose.

**Missing Person**

Charlotte was to meet up with Julia in the city and be home by 10:00 p.m. at the latest. My husband and I get home at 11:30. She's not there. For the first time ever there has been no phone call, no message, nothing.

I call Julia's parents, the Andersons, but I can't get through. Their line is busy, busy, busy. I call AT&T to verify the call.

"You're calling from a phone booth. We can't verify the call," the operator tells me.

"I'm not calling from a phone booth. I'm calling from my home."

"I'll give you to my supervisor."

"This is your AT&T supervisor." Verifying the call costs $10.81. But I am told again that I can't verify the number anyway because I am calling from a phone booth. Idiots! I'm starting to get frantic.

I'm not worried that she's dead or kidnapped, but I am worried about what this means in the scheme of things. Will this be the first of many disobediences? Is this the beginning of the end? Is this, in fact, The End of My Control? Then I remember The Tattoo, and I think, what control?

I stop worrying for a moment and jump to The Big Question. What should her punishment be? By planning her punishment, I calm myself with the false sense of having regained control.

Suddenly, I have a theory: she didn't call or leave a message because she got her tongue pierced after all, and I would be able to tell this immediately by how she sounds on the phone.

I call her friend Holly. She doesn't know where Charlotte is either. She's been trying to reach her all day. She is worried. And I am now on the verge of tears. I'm in the middle of filling my missing person's report.

"She's five feet, five inches tall, 130 pounds. Long black hair. Identifiable markings include a tattoo of an Irish witch symbol, multiple ear piercings, and a possible tongue stud."

Finally, I get through to the Andersons. Mr. Anderson is obviously tired and possibly annoyed at being bothered by what to him must seem like the most minor of infractions given what he's gone through with his two little felon daughters.

"Oh, the girls got the 11:07. They should be getting in now," he says. Minutes later the phone rings. It's Charlotte. Her voice sounds normal and unstudded.

"Where are you?" I say. Immediately she lies.

"We were at Holly's. I didn't get your message" I am so delighted to catch her in this lie, I'm no longer angry. In fact, from the time I hear her voice, I'm not angry at all. I would've only been angry at this point if she had actually gotten herself killed. Now I have the real joy of confronting her.

"You weren't at Holly's because I talked to Holly just a few minutes ago, and she hasn't seen you all day. Why are you lying?"

There is only the slightest pause, and then she launches into the real story. "I didn't want to worry you."

"Where are you?"

"We're at the diner."

"How did you get to the diner?"

"A taxi."

"Come home."

"Now? But we're hungry." I can't believe that after all this she is trying to negotiate a later curfew.

"Charlotte, now."

Tucker and I discuss punishment.

"Why don't you ask her what punishment she thinks would be appropriate," he suggests. I've heard of this approach before. It sounds very fair. Very forgiving. God has smiled down on me and saved my child. I am open to anything, even fairness and forgiveness.

She is home within fifteen minutes. I do the one thing I told Tucker not to do. "Show me your tongue," I say. She does. There is no sign of a stud.

Then I give her the what-do-you-think-would-be-an-appropriate-punishment speech.

"I don't know," she says.

"Well, think about it and get back to me." I hug her once. Then I hug her a second time. She can't wait to escape.

*Cousins, cousins, cousins. Charlotte, 2nd from left front row.*

Charlotte learns to drive (out of my life).

# Learner's Permit

**Counting Days**

"I've got only 209 days until I get my learner's permit," Charlotte announces.

How could this be? Hadn't she just learned to walk across the room without falling and knocking out a baby tooth? How could she suddenly be old enough to drive? Where had the time gone? Where had her baby teeth gone?

Only 209 days of my driving her the two miles to school.

This is my plan: to record what she says during every one of the rides we have left together. I will get her to talk about herself. Years from now she'll thank me for recording this precious time in her life.

I forget that she's fifteen years old, it's 7:30 in the morning, and she hates me.

We get in the car, and I start off with some simple questions just to get her warmed up:

"What's your favorite color, Charlotte?"

"I don't know."

"There must be one color that you like more than others."

"Okay. Green. And blue." I am very encouraged.

"Good. Good. What's your favorite food?"

"I don't know."

"You like pizza, right?"

"Okay. Pizza."

Time is running out. We're almost there. I'm feeling slightly panicky. "So, what's your favorite time of year?"

"Spring and winter," she answers all too quickly. I know she's lying. I know she prefers summer. I try a shotgun approach. "Who's your favorite actor, singer, rapper?"

"I hate these questions. If you're going to ask me questions, why don't you ask me something important?"

"Like what, honey?"

"Like, have I had sex? Do I use protection? Do I do drugs? What kind of drugs do I do? If you're going to ask me questions, at least make them interesting."

I gulp. "Let's get back to green and blue. Which of those two colors do you prefer?"

**The Written Test**

Charlotte gets eight out of ten correct on the written driving test, which means she passed. She gets behind the wheel of what is now "our" car.

The next morning, when it comes time to drive her to her PSAT course, I automatically start to get into the driver's side of the car. She waves me away. She drives us downtown.

"How do I change lanes?" she asks, suddenly worried. That makes two of us.

"Don't," I advise. "Wait. Go around the block."

Instead of taking me straight home, Charlotte drives me to Cumberland Farms to get herself a frappucino. This new, sophisticated drink must have something to do with her new, sophisticated life as a driver.

"Do you know how dumb it feels to be driven around like this?" I say, impatient to get home, where I have work to do.

"Now you know how I've felt for the past sixteen years," she replies.

**The First Accident?**

We are driving on Post Road, and a car starts to turn into the Citibank shopping center right in front of us. Charlotte doesn't slow down. We are going to hit this car.

This will be her first accident, and I'm glad to be here to comfort her during what will no doubt be an upsetting experience. We are rushing toward the car's rear end. What will be will be, I think, as long as it doesn't affect her ability to get her license or increase our present insurance rates.

The other car is still slowly turning, and we are going at the same speed as we were before.

We miss the car's rear bumper by an inch.

"Sorry, sorry, sorry," Charlotte says, laughing nervously. "I meant to put my foot on the brake, but I didn't."

I shake my head. We are both reminded of how easy it is to crash into something when you forget little things like putting your foot on the brake. Also, we both remember that she is just learning to drive.

**Car Talk**

Charlotte, having only just gotten her learner's permit, is already shopping for a car. She calls a number she sees on the back of a Cabriolet parked on the street. She talks to a "really nice girl named Lisa". Anyone who is going to aid Charlotte in realizing her dream of owning a car is already "really nice" without even having to lift a finger. She makes an appointment the next day to look at the 57,000-mile car "for only $5,000."

I get behind the wheel of the Cabriolet because we have agreed beforehand that to have Charlotte drive a shift car for the first time in front of a stranger would be a big mistake. We drive to a deserted area and change places.

She stops, she starts, she never gets out of second gear. When she shifts, she keeps the gas going so the car makes a terrible gasping sound.

Kachuh kachuh kachuh.

I feel like the Eternally Patient Mother: kind and supportive beyond belief. This is good for Charlotte. And it's really good for me to see that I can be this way.

"I don't think it's worth the money she's asking," I say to get her off the hook and out of second gear.

Charlotte quickly decides she doesn't want a shift car after all, so it turns out to be a very successful first test drive.

**The First Time on the Highway**

Charlotte has been putting this off. It is only from exit 18 to exit 22, but it is on I-95, notorious for its big, fast trucks and numerous fatalities. I realize I am pushing her to do this because I want to be there for another of her firsts.

"This is scary," she says, as she edges onto the highway. Cars are zipping behind us, and I am at a real loss as to how to explain merging to her. I myself never knew if you were supposed to slow down to let the merging car in, speed up so that the driver has to enter the lane after you, or stubbornly maintain your speed—even though it looks as if you're headed for a collision.

I feel as if I have taken her out in a tippy rowboat and suddenly remembered that neither of us knows how to swim.

"Go! Go! Go!" I finally shout. She jams on the accelerator, and we shoot out into our lane. The driver who we have just cut off honks at us. Charlotte ducks her head in embarrassment, and I flip the finger at the angry driver.

**License Pick-up Day**

Just as I feared, the day Charlotte gets her license is here.

Of course, Charlotte brought her friend Fifi with her, so the moment is not even our moment. It belongs to Charlotte and Fifi.

Charlotte, Miss Meticulous, has just noticed that they forgot to put "restrictive lenses" on her license. She has an invalid license. Oh good, she can't drive. We can all go home and go back to where we were: Mom, Dad, and Little Girl. Maybe I can dig out her old Aprica stroller, stuff her in, and wheel her right back to babyhood.

"What's the difference?" Fifi asks.

Charlotte explains: "This says I have perfect vision, which I don't."

"Forget it, it's okay," Fifi says.

But for Charlotte, it's definitely not okay. She wants this, her first license, to follow the exact letter of the law. She gets back into line to have her license corrected. She has to have her picture taken again, which is too bad, because the first one turns out to be much better.

**Dinner with the Parents**

Charlotte drives us to and from a restaurant. Even though she has her driver's license, she still depends on us for food. Tucker sits in the backseat. I sit up front with her.

On our way home a boy driving a gold Isuzu in the lane next to us spots Charlotte. He speeds up. He waits for her. When she pulls up alongside, he speeds up again. She giggles and catches up with him. She turns up Green Day. She taps the wheel with her purple frosted nails. She is beautiful. She is cool. She has her wheels and the night and the music.

She also has her mother and father stuffed in the car with her. But for a moment she is able to transcend this little detail.

Charlotte and the Isuzu boy continue down Post Road in tandem, performing the classic car-mating dance: quick eye contact, followed by cool indifference, then a thrust of the accelerator, followed by a subtle braking. Finally, he speeds on. There are no goodbyes and no regrets.

She turns off Post Road and onto the once-dreaded I-95. Her perfectly tanned arm rests casually on the open window. Her long hair billows back like a dark silk scarf. She is her own car commercial. She is, most definitely, licensed to drive.

*My little mother is on the left in the gathering of sylphs.*

# Little Mother

My father called her "Little Mother," which she hated and which is why he called her that. Little mother came from the fact that she was short, five foot, two. But it also had to do with the fact that she took up very little emotional space. She was undemanding and infuriatingly unselfish. She was not quite the "It's okay, I'll sit in the dark" kind of mother, but she came very close.

My mother was a very big sewer and knitter. She knitted me heavy-duty ski sweaters that would have been perfect for surviving at the North Pole. She sewed patchwork place mats and aprons for me. I never wear the aprons, but I use her place mats almost every day. They are starting to wear out. I've often wished I could give my daughter something to remember me by. But I'm not a knitter, a sewer, or a place mat maker.

She was a big dealer in practical tips. She literally gave me words to live by—not always profound, but they were useful nonetheless.

"Horizontal stripes tend to broaden you."

"Put on slippers, or you'll catch cold."

"Mayonnaise takes water stains out of wood."

"If you punish a dog with a newspaper, it teaches him to hate the paper boy."

"If you don't put binding tape on seams, they tend to fray."

"If you shave your legs, the hair grows back faster."

I realize that I remember many of her words but none of her feelings. How did my mother feel about the day I came home with a failure notice in algebra? I remember how I felt. I was ashamed, devastated, and fearful about any future I might have. And I remember her telling me that it was okay even if I failed. All she asked of me was that I try. And if I tried my best and failed, well, that was okay.

But how did she really feel underneath all her kind, comforting words? Was she worried that this was just the beginning of many failures in my life? First algebra, then geometry, then, God forbid, The Big Typing Test? Did she expect so little of me because she hadn't expected very much of herself? I don't know; she never talked about herself. In those days, in the '50s, talking about feelings just wasn't done. Basically, feelings were something to be a little hidden and a little embarrassed about. Like sex.

My mother was a big collector. She collected other people's recipes, shoes on sale, buttons, something called bric-a-brac, fabric swatches (thus the reason for the patchwork place mats and aprons), pieces of driftwood—all sorts of odds and ends that she was always going to use to "make something."

"Mom, what do you want with all these corks?"

"Oh, I'll use them."

"But for what?"

You could see her mind working, mentally flipping through the millions of Good Housekeeping Arts & Crafts articles to come up with the one ingenuous project that required 5,000 corks in assorted sizes. That Christmas she created a collection of cork jewelry: necklaces, dangling earrings, bracelets, all covered in blue and green glitter.

My little mother was a big do-it-yourselfer. She stained the pine panels in our basement and, as a result, came down with an infection of the gums because of the toxic exposure to the shoe polish she used. Yes, she went through hundreds of little bottles of oxblood shoe polish, using the dabber to stain the walls, turning what once was a rumpus room into a real, authentic redwood den, redwood being all the rage in the '50s. In the same house in Denver, she built a cinder block wall in the backyard, figuring out how to level the blocks on slanted ground, mixing her own cement, enduring my father's funny comments when he came home from the office and stood, head cocked, holding his before-dinner Scotch.

There was nothing she couldn't do, except grow taller, although she tried. She had a huge collection of sample size shoes that she got on sale. Sample sizes (size five and a half) were always cheaper. She wore a size six. So, of course, the shoes always gave her bunions, and she ultimately gave up wearing them.

Feelings were not something worth collecting. She didn't hold grudges, she didn't get angry, she didn't talk about sadness or happiness or resentment or joy. I don't know what she felt about a lot of things. As her daughter, I can guess, and I think my guesses are pretty good, but I don't know for sure. She kept it all to herself.

I happen to think that's what gave her cancer in the end. Of course, the cigarettes didn't help. My mother was a very big inhaler.

She had one small request when she died and that was to cremate her. She had always made a point of reminding us that was what she wanted. Her ashes were put in a little urn in a little box in a small square hole in a big cemetery in Denver. My little mother, true to herself, took up the smallest possible space, even in death.

*My mother, Pearl Ethel Spring's engagement picture.*

*My little mother with little me.*

*My mother made all my clothes.*

# Mother-Daughter Outfits

Clothes were always both a huge bond and a potential battle for my mother, my daughter, and me. What I learned over the years when getting into discussions with them about our wardrobes was how very hard it was for me to be honest.

**New York City, 1975**

I am living and working in the fashion capital of the world. A box of clothes arrives from my mother in Denver, clothes she has sewn. She has been making clothes for me since before I was born. I open the box.

A corduroy skirt. With box pleats and rickrack trim. It makes me look like I weigh 300 pounds. Also a pink velvet jumper with straps that crisscross in the back.

No one I know has worn a jumper like this since graduating from the sixth grade. What they're wearing these days in the Big Apple are miniskirts and high stacked boots.

I call my mother to thank her, and while the phone is ringing, I try to think up something nice to say because "If you can't say anything nice … "

"Hey, Mom, I got the clothes."

"Tell me what you think. Really. Be honest. You won't hurt my feelings." This is her standard refrain.

Maybe this is my big chance to get her to stop sewing for me. My closet is crammed with clothes that she's made that I can't get rid of because when she comes to visit, she always wants to see me in them. I'm twenty-five years old. It's time for this charade to end. I take a deep breath.

"Okay. Mom, the skirt is too big and makes me look really fat."

Silence.

"And I can't wear pink. It's my worst color." Silence.

"Mom, you wanted me to be honest." Silence.

"Mom? Are you still there?"

"I thought you loved pink. You told me you got so much wear out of that pink pantsuit I made for you. It took me forever to line it."

"I only wore it once. I'm sorry." Silence.

"Please, Mom, don't be hurt."

"I'm not hurt. I'm happy we're having this conversation. I'm glad you're being honest with me. I'm just sorry I wasted all that good corduroy. And the pink velvet … it's a shame. I hate to waste good fabric, not to mention the rickrack."

My mother's signature detail is rickrack.

"Oh, I loved the rickrack. Did I mention that? It's really cute rickrack."

"Well, maybe you can rip it off the skirt and sew it on something you like better. Oh, I forgot. You don't sew. You just pay department store prices for clothes that aren't even lined."

"Mom, please. Oh, wait a second. I think I had the skirt on backward. Let me put it on again. Oh, it's great. Silly me; I had the whole thing on wrong. I actually love it."

"You're just saying that."

"No, really. I mean it."

My mother died twenty-seven years ago. I still have that pink jumper hanging in my closet somewhere, as if she is going to pop in someday and want to see how it looks on me. But I also keep it around to show my friends how beautifully my mother sewed.

**Westport, Connecticut, 1999**

"I love weekends because then I get to dress skanky." My fifteen-year-old daughter, Charlotte, shares this piece of information with me on one of those rare occasions when she feels like telling me a little something about herself. She shows me what she means by dressing skanky.

Her black slinky, shiny, skintight pants are rolled down two inches below her waist, revealing her rhinestone belly button jewelry. My black lace bra, which I had given her because it didn't fit me, is a demitasse for her latte grande breasts. Over the bra is stretched a barely buttoned glittery, metallic black, can't-get-much-tighter-than-this Betsy Johnson cardigan. On her feet are four-inch strappy heels. Her chest, her cheeks, and her neck are awash in sparkle or glitter or whatever it is they call it.

"What do you think?" Charlotte says, holding out her arms and putting added stress on the cardigan's mother-of-pearl buttons.

Was this a challenge or just a question?

"Gorgeous! Fabulous!" I enthuse and then immediately feel like a complete hypocrite. The outfit is slutsville. It is trouble. What kind of mother am I? Where are my motherly standards? Where's my sense of decency? Where's my honesty?

I'll tell you; they're lost in my tremendous need to be her friend, to have her like me, just for moment. Realizing this, and realizing the hopelessness of my goal, I take a deep breath and rework my response. I try, perhaps for the last time, to be honest about clothes.

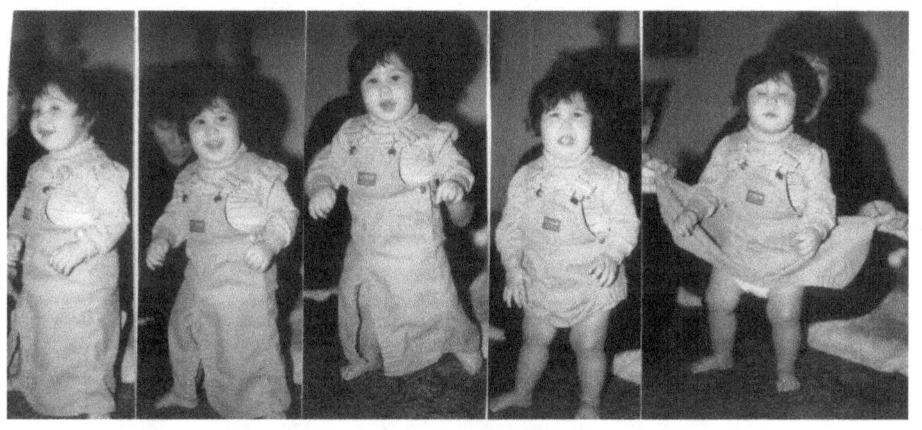

*Charlotte makes pink overalls into a fashion statement..*

"Charlotte, as your mother, I just want to go on record as saying that this is an attack outfit. Boys see this, and they will want to attack you."

"Oh, I know." She smiles, acknowledging the rightness of my remark. What she is saying is, You idiot, this is the dress code. I'm supposed to walk around looking like a Las Vegas showgirl.

I have to confess there is a part of me that really does think she looks fabulous and gorgeous. I love the fact that she is proud of her body. Why shouldn't she wear her top down to here and her skirts up to there? After all, we live in a town where every single girl her age dresses exactly the same way. It is an entire community of Madonna look-alikes.

And I certainly understand the need to dress like everyone else. It was something I was forever arguing with my mother about when I was Charlotte's age.

"Joan Jilka has a skirt just like this," I told my mother, pointing out a skirt at Neusteter's in Denver. (I have no idea what we were shopping for at the time, since my mother could sew everything better and cheaper than anything I might want to buy in a department store.) I thought the fact that Joan Jilka got straight A's would convince my mother that this skirt—a skirt that was so shoddily made, according to her, it "didn't even have a rolled hem"—was worth the investment. It wasn't. She made me the same skirt complete with a rolled hem, but hers was lined in silk.

I still think about that pink velvet jumper. Maybe I'll get Charlotte to try it on one day, just for laughs. She doesn't know how lucky she is that I never learned how to sew.

*My treasured girl.*

# The Birthday Card

It is the day before my birthday; Charlotte and I have one of those run-ins that make me wonder how low I can go. We are standing in line at CVS to pay for a gift for her swim team buddy.

"Oh, and I have to get you a birthday card," she says, as if she's talking about shampoo or Q-tips. It seems I can't not make an issue of this. It starts out funny but quickly deteriorates into what I'm really feeling, which is terribly hurt.

A woman standing ahead of us in line keeps looking over at me. She is not laughing at my dialed up clever, ironic comments. Oh no, she is giving me a look of complete sympathy. My feelings are showing all over my face. They are drawing attention to themselves like a pair of really ugly earrings.

"Oh great," I say. "You probably want me to pay for my own birthday card, too." I mean it to come out funny, and it falls flat. Again, the woman shoots me a look. To make matters worse, Charlotte keeps turning to me and saying:

"What? What? Why are you so mad?"

I am silent now. I am desperate to preserve whatever shred of dignity I have left. The cashier is incredibly slow. I just want to take my hurt feelings and go out and sit in the car. But I have to stand there, awkward and angry, feeling like some misunderstood adolescent.

"How do you think I feel?" I say to her once we get in the car. "How would you feel if it were your birthday, and I said that?" I repeated the birthday card line to her.

"I didn't say it that way," Charlotte says, clearly feeling misrepresented. "I was just reminding myself out loud.""Listen, I'm a human being just like you, and I care about my birthday just as much as you care about yours, and it hurts my feelings when you treat it like that." The more I express myself, the angrier I get. "Don't get me a card. I don't want a card. I don't want anything." The only thing that keeps me from crying is I have to see to drive.

I was definitely over the edge. I thought about my mother and how, when asked what she wanted for her birthday, she would say things like "I don't want anything, just your love." Or "Just for you to do well in school." Or "Just for you to watch what you eat." Talk about hard to buy for. Over the years I would buy her stuff, and a year or two later I would get the gift back.

"Here, this will look much better on you than on me," she would say.

Again and again I would feel as if I had failed. Failed to guess the right gift. Failed to express the right love. Failed to be the right kind of daughter.

As soon as we get home, I go on bluefly.com and show Charlotte the exact black pashmina shawl for $125 that she and her father can order for me for my birthday. Forget the card.

*Charlotte continues to give me joy.*

*Invading Charlotte's space, as usual.*

# The Invasion of Privacy Issue

**Watching versus Spying**

I see a white Audi drive up, circle around the driveway, and park behind the tall rhododendrons, where I can't see who it is. All I know is that it's someone who's brought Charlotte home from school. I immediately imagine this picture in my head: Charlotte kissing this stranger goodbye; tongue kissing someone I can't see; getting pregnant from and exchanging dirty needles with a nameless, faceless stranger who drives a white Audi.

I jump up from the computer and run to my bedroom window for a better view. I see her getting out of the backseat, politely saying thanks for the ride to a boy I don't know who is wearing a heavy-duty silver nose ring and has a shaved head. I hide so she doesn't catch a glimpse of me looking out the window and quickly tiptoe back to my office so it looks as though I never left, never even dreamed of spying on her.

"Who gave you a ride?" I ask very casually. "Chuck," she says.

"Who's Chuck?" "He's a senior."

"Oh, okay," I say, not exactly satisfied but thinking, albeit ludicrously, if he was a senior in high school (a very difficult high school), then he couldn't possibly be a dirty needle-using, impregnating, gang-leading skinhead, could he? Also, there was the fact that she had been sitting in the backseat, not in the front. How much needle exchanging and impregnating could have gone on?

**Observing versus Snooping**

It is just after the Columbine High School shooting incident. All day on NPR the talk is of parents' responsibilities. Are they responsible? How do they help their kids get through these terrible teenage times? The bottom line from the callers and experts is that parents are responsible and have to make it a point to know what's going on with their kids. Translated, I take this to mean yes, it is okay to spy on your children. It is okay to read diaries, to search drawers, to call them at their friends' houses, to follow them in cars and down dark alleys littered with dirty needles.

The whole concept of respecting their privacy flies out the window when you suspect bad stuff is going on, so I am fighting the urge to go into Charlotte's room and search it. I realize that what I would be searching for are her secrets. Doesn't she have a right to her private life as well as her privacy?

Plus, she isn't showing any signs of aberrant behavior. Her grades are okay. Her tongue is still unpierced, her nose still ringless and studless. She adheres to the curfew, the rule of no parties when we are away. She calls us when she is going to be late. She says she doesn't do drugs or drink. She doesn't smoke, she says. She acts for all intents and purposes like a well-behaved kid. She is for all intents and purposes a well-behaved kid. So, why do I worry?

Because I know all the stuff I did as a kid. Of course, I never really broke the law. Well, that's not true. I did steal. I shoplifted. But it was small stuff from the 5&10: Hazel Bishop Persian melon lipstick, costume jewelry, mustard seed necklaces, dainty chain anklets, and chrome-plated ID bracelets. I stole candy. I stole money from my parents for candy. And I lied. Lying came as naturally to me as stealing. In my code of ethics, if you were going to steal, you had to lie. It just made sense.

My mother: "Where did you get that mustard seed necklace?" Me: "It was a gift from Judy Weaver."

My mother: "She just gave it to you? It's not even your birthday." Me: "She had two of them, so she gave me one."

So I come up with a very good excuse to go into Charlotte's room: I need to retrieve our community tweezers.

Suddenly, I see a strange apparatus on her bookshelf, a small oblong object. It has a place for air to go in on one side and out through the top. It is clear plastic and has some sort of black material inside.

I immediately think: drugs, hashish, used crack cocaine, or something exotic and newly on the scene. Maybe this is what Ecstasy looks like. I go from wondering what kind of drug it is to thinking, How could she leave it out like this. How could she be so, so stupid? Then I think, *maybe it belongs to one of her friends*. Sigh of relief.

Still, her friend or friends are using it in her room probably with her knowledge. Again, a sharp intake of breath. And then I see there is a name on the side of the object. I go and get my glasses so I can read what it says: Sweater Defuzzer. The black stuff inside is nothing more than defuzzed fuzz balls from one of Charlotte's sweaters. I laugh. And then I think, can this be inhaled?

# Eight Stories by Lisa Maxwell

*Footloose*

*Mr. Yarn Man*

*Step into My Office*

*The Birth*

*The Incinerator*

*Pea-Pee*

*Born Atheist*

*The Goddess*

*Me, perpetually barefoot, with my brother Gray, in Nantucket 1967.*

# *Footloose*

Having grown up in both a time and a place that shoes didn't matter, well, shoes didn't matter.

When I was of the age that girls begin to develop serious emotional relationships with their footwear, it was the late '60's and early '70's, and bare feet (for as long into the season as one could be barefooted) were the style. Plus, it was very much a doable style during my summers in Nantucket. I rode my bike, hitchhiked, drove, baby sat, housecleaned, walked up and down cobblestoned Main Street, hung out, danced, and drank in bars shoe-less.

My mother would turn away at the sight of my blackened soles and dirty toenails and shake her head, prompting me to "put on some shoes!" knowing that I wouldn't and that they would eventually get cleaned by seawater or the occasional shower.

The one place where this was strictly verboten was the Nantucket Yacht Club.

"NO BARE FEET", read the unavoidable, discreetly printed sign as one entered the mullioned double doors.

My equally defiant friend and I would dare the proclamation and come sniggering in, walking down the smooth, impeccably waxed wood floors holding one shoe in each hand, waiting to be challenged, which we always were. My bare feet stood for my rebellious nature for many summers. They were my signature.

Times changed, seasons passed, and I ended up first in college in Italy (the shoe capital of the world), then art school in New York City (the shoe capital of the USA). Shoe lust was inevitable, a rite of passage from hippie girlhood to young-and-confused womanhood. During my senior year a girlfriend had the coveted job of working as a salesgirl at Charles Jourdan Shoes on Fifth Avenue, *the* shoe store in New York at the time. I became obsessed with the shoes and would count the days leading up to the spring, fall, and after-Christmas sales. I was waitressing and making enough money to buy them on sale, with her employee discount.

I soon assembled a closet full of exclusively Charles Jourdan super-high heels, which, when I began my career in 1977 at age twenty-one, became my signature. Now my mother would watch perplexedly as I teetered down the platform at the Westport train station coming home for weekend visits.

"How can you walk in those things, Lizzie?" she'd ask. I'd just smile. I never saw my mother, who was a solid five foot three to my five foot seven, wearing anything over an inch in height on her feet. When she died, many of the shoes she had in my pubescence were still there in her closet.

As time passed I found myself flip-flopping more and more between craving the latest-coolest-ludicrously-high-must-have style and the innate desire for comfort and practicality that my mother knew all along.

As life tends to go full-cycle, happily I am back enjoying the utter unadorned freedom I have wearing plain old bare feet.

A lame attempt at modelling, in my Charles Jourdan heels, 1978.

*My mother with all four of us, (me on the right). Always a handful.*

# Mr. Yarn Man

Amazingly, my mother found the time to both knit and sew. Considering that she had one, then two, then three, then four children in a span of ten years, just keeping track of us seems Herculean to me now.

She made us clothes—matching dresses for the three girls and sometimes even something for herself and my baby brother. She was an excellent seamstress and taught each one of us how to sew as best as we could given our respective ages. The sewing machine was an ancient Singer, small and black with gold trim, and it never failed.

I was fascinated by all of the sewing paraphernalia. There were the bobbins, the needles, and the different feet that got changed, depending on which type of stitching you wanted to produce, by lifting the lever, unscrewing the piece, and replacing it with another funny-looking one—for zippers, let's say. There was the pedal, which I could barely reach. And the thump… thump…thump sound I loved, which varied depending on how wide the stitches were and the thickness of the fabric. Then the whirrrrr when you came around the straightaway of a long seam. My mother was masterful at feeding the fabric and stepping on the gas with just the right pressure.

The state of her sewing table would vary between immaculate and totally disarrayed, depending on where she was with a project. I volunteered often to tidy it up, which I loved doing, organizing all the thread by weight, color, and size, lining up the packages of pins and needles, snaps, hooks and eyes, zippers, ribbons, elastic, thimbles, pincushions, and scissors. I marveled at the pinking shears. How on earth did they make them with that zigzagged edge? Also, there were her prized razor-sharp sewing scissors, which she used to snip open seams. A curious little scarecrow-type figure made out of yarn dangled from one of the finger loops of these scissors.

"You must always mark sharp objects so that nobody hurts themselves by grabbing the wrong end and poking themselves," my mother informed me.

"Ohhhh," I said while examining the funny figure. That made a lot of sense. It worked, too. I always knew which end of those scissors to grab when combing through the drawers in her sewing table to find them. I never once poked my finger on their points.

I acquired those scissors at some point in my adulthood. The original yarn man was lost, but he'd been replaced by another one my mother made while passing time sitting on her bed after she had been stricken with emphysema, the disease that would slowly, over ten years, take her life.

Those scissors came to live in a silver jar in my bathroom among miscellaneous makeup brushes, emery boards, eyeliner pencils, tweezers, and the like.

My son, Lake, would take them for various tasks even as a little boy. I explained to him what my mother had explained to me when he first giggled at the sight of the little man.

"You must always mark sharp objects so that nobody hurts themselves by grabbing the wrong end and poking themselves," reciting my mother's words

"Ohhhh," he said.

In 2004 Lake, my husband, George, and I went on a trip to Europe. Without thinking, I put the scissors, along with some other toiletries, into my handbag. In the wake of 9/11, they were, of course, immediately spotted by a security agent at the airport.

"We are going to have to confiscate these, ma'am," the agent announced, holding them up, the little man dangling.

What!? My heart stopped. I don't know whose face was more horrified, Lake's or mine. That little guy meant everything to us.

Thinking fast I blurted "Uhhh, umm, uhh, well, okay, I understand, but umm, well … can I remove the little yarn figure? PLEEEEESE?"

Being a reasonable sort he replied "Yes, ma'am, that would be okay."

Oh, THANK GOD! I screamed to myself.

Together Lake and I nervously extracted the object, carefully untying it from the scissors, which were then tossed into a bin with hundreds of other sharp metal no-no's. I hurriedly stuffed the little man into my purse. He was saved.

When we got home, I dug out another pair of scissors from the remains of my mother's sewing things, ones that weren't nearly as special, and attached Mr. Yarn Man to them, where he lives today. He serves much more as a tribute to my mother and her infinite practicality and wisdom than to the long-lost craft of sewing.

*Mr. Yarn Man, safe at home today.*

*Me, (2nd from right) with my sister and cousins in happier times at my kitchen table.*

# Pea-Pee

The family was assembled for dinner in the dining room. My father was home this evening, which was why we weren't eating in the kitchen. He sat at the head of the large oval table to my right. My sisters, Anne and Linda, were across from me, and my baby brother was in a high chair at the table. He had already been fed and was in his own little world, oblivious.

The meal, though formal, was going normally, the conversation was routine.

"Anne, tell your father about school today," said my mother. Anne was biting her nails, a habit my father loathed.

"Get your hands out of your mouth," he ordered disgustedly.

My father was a daunting presence and was utterly intolerant of any aberrant behavior at the table, which was always set perfectly by one of us three girls. There we would be, napkins in our laps, backs ramrod straight, legs crossed ladylike at our ankles.

We were, of course, expected to eat everything on our plates. I was little enough to be sitting in a high chair, with my plate resting on the plastic tray. Linda had chimed in by now, talking enthusiastically about *her* accomplishments of the day. I was drifting off, becoming preoccupied with my peas. Hard as I tried, I couldn't keep them from rolling off my fork.

The commands were replaying silently in my head. "Don't stab at your food!"

"Never use your hands as a pusher!" "Bring your food to your mouth!"

I slid my fork carefully under four or five peas, and with as steady a hand as possible I attempted to bring them to my mouth, my eyes all the while fixated on the fork. I was totally engrossed in this task when suddenly my father slammed his hand down on the table and snapped me out of my daydreaming.

"Elizabeth! Stop playing with your food," he barked.

I jumped, the peas flew off the fork, and I became painfully aware of all the eyes that were glaring at me. Apparently, everyone else was finished eating.

The words, "Ooops. Sorry, Dad." unable to come out of my mouth would never suffice.

Humiliated, face burning red, I put on a brave smile and began the process again.

"On the count of one… two… three…" my father commanded.

I gripped my fork and slid it under the now cold, hard, round culprits. Slowly, slowly, oh so carefully, I negotiated each one onto the curved tines.

Momentary success! Four or five in one try.

Now began the agonizing journey to my mouth. My arm stiffened, and with all eyes watching, in terror I raised the fork. I flinched.

The peas came tumbling down in slow motion, as my father backed his chair away from the table with a loud thump. He was behind me before the peas hit the plate, a giant, enraged man. Without a word he picked up the high chair with me in it and stomped into the kitchen, slamming it down at the kitchen table so hard that all the dishes bounced up and all the remaining peas went flying onto the floor. He turned and marched into the living room. I felt the warm fluid fill my underwear as the pee trickled down my leg. I was not fit to be present in the dining room any longer that evening.

*Baby Lake, 1993.*

# The Birth
## (To my son, Lake)

We arrived at the hospital by cab around 2 a.m. By 10:00 a.m. the strange, furiously painful feelings had caused me to surrender to the not-so-natural-but-who-cares-at-this-point epidural.

"Fine, yes, no problem, yup, I'm sure, yes ... JUST DO IT!!!!"

Time inched along, people shuffled in and out, needles were prepped, contractions erupted, and much higher up than I thought, not in my vagina, thank you very much. I cursed all those dumb Lamaze classes. I wasn't prepared for this. I had no comprehension of what was happening. There was no sync to my breathing, no earth mom feelings. It was all a lie!

I lay around, waiting and waiting, contracting and contracting. The needle was inserted.

"Okay, take a deep breath ... you might feel a pinch."

"OWWWWWWWWWWWWWWWW!!"

I looked at the clock: 11:00, 12:00, 1:00 p.m. I made some phone calls. "Yes, I am in labor... for hours... since 2:00 in the morning!" I told my sister.

Any time now!

Your father, went out to get some lunch.

Enough time had passed from when my water broke that there was some growing concern about infection. There was talk about inducing labor. What? What does that mean? Are they talking about me? I was the only one giving birth in the room. Must be. It was like watching a movie, 2:00, 3:00, 4:00 p.m. Finally, it was rock and roll time.

I don't remember if I was induced or not. I do remember that the epidural was not doing what it was paid to do.

Pain. Screaming.

Why on earth do they always show women in labor on their back and spread-eagled? That's no way to have a baby. You have to bear down, like you do when you are taking that giant you-know-what, and your face goes red, and your eyes bug out and tear.

NO ONE TOLD ME THAT! That's where the REAL no-pussy-footing-around pushing comes from. That's right. You get up on all fours. That makes MUCH more sense. You have SO much more power.

Jesus. I thought you were supposed to push from your stomach muscles. NO! IT'S FROM YOUR BOWELS, YOU IDIOT!!

So up and over I went.

OWWWWWWWWWWWWW. SHIT, OH MY GOD, OWWW.

I'm squeezing someone's hand. Whose hand? Contractions. More contractions. That rolling pain was now dialed up to the max and just kept coming.

Those god damn movies, those god damn classes! They prey on pregnant women! Either that or women prey on them. So self-indulgent!! My God, women have been squatting since Croesus. It comes with the territory, babe! I DIDN'T LEARN ANYTHING! THE NERVE OF THEM TAKING MY UNREIMBURSED-BY-INSURANCE $350 AND SHOW ME A BUNCH OF CRAP!

Suddenly, I felt the rock-hard crown of the head beginning to emerge. You gotta be kidding! That thing was SO hard! Then, PUSH, PUSH, PUSH.

Blurrrpppppp...this THING plopped out.

That's exactly what it felt like—this big thing just plopped out.

I did not want to look. I was conditioned not to look. See, in those classes, when they showed those films of the baby right after it came out, it was BLUE! And WRITHING. And horrible looking.

I knew MY baby was fine, and that he would be fine, but I JUST DIDN'T WANT TO SEE A BLUE FACE. Not after all that! Clean him up first, okay?

I turned my head away, but then in an instant, and of course by instinct, I turned back. And there you were. It was 4:40 p.m

Your face wasn't blue, baby. It was pink and soft and happy and healthy and little and warm and moist and fat cheeked. YAY!! You weren't blue! No, not at all! Not your face or your little perfect body or anything!

That perfect thing came out of ME?

Then came the afterbirth, the placenta. This next thing plopped out. It looked like a giant liver. EEEEEWWWWW. It was definitely from another planet. What the…!!! Good God. No one told me about THAT!

I bled a lot, apparently more than usual. There was a lot of shuffling around, masked faces and gloved hands shoving things in and around me. Eventually, the bleeding stopped.

Your father and I still hadn't agreed on a name for you. Actually, we hadn't ever agreed on anything. That's why we weren't married. There were five or six names pending. I was too worn out to argue.

Soon you and I were both cleaned up. I don't remember if I was in pain or out of pain. It didn't matter. There you were, in my arms, smelling like fresh baby, wrapped tightly in the utilitarian scrubbed cotton hospital blanket with the little newborn blue-and-white hat on your head, pink-faced, full-lipped, and, most incredibly, for real.

My memories are hazy. I stayed overnight. They brought you in. They took you away. I sort of tried breast-feeding. I think I was uncomfortable. Then sometime in the morning, I went to this manditory breast-feeding how-to class. Yeah, yeah, okay, right. Hmm, that's interesting. Not really. Pump demonstrations. Pictures of inverted nipples. "Beware… this could happen to you." Demonstrations of how to rub cream on your breasts. Contented moms, contented babies. I pretended that I got it all and that I would follow everything to a "T". I wanted to, but just like with reading those baby books, I knew I would retain virtually nothing. Oh well.

My parents came. They held you. Your dad's sister came. She met mom and dad for the first time. In fact, it was the first time ever the two families had interacted. My father remembers Grace fondly. "She was a class act," he always said. They would meet briefly only once more twelve years later, eight years after mom's death, at your bar mitzvah. Your dad's family did not come to your christening at the Church of the Incarnation nine months after your birth.

I gathered you up, Lake, at that moment called Willie, short for William. By the time we left the hospital, you had five other names on your birth certificate. (Lake William Julian Bayard Tucker Wolosker). Are you kidding me? Even though I had no obligation to, I gave you your dad's surname. It seemed like the right thing to do.

I also gathered up all the free stuff I could manage: diapers, little samples of petroleum jelly, a whole case of four-ounce glass formula bottles, envelopes mostly filled with coupons for really ugly nursing bras and child development toys and educational videos for babies and Parents magazine and the like. We three, you, your dad, and I, got into a cab. It was a cold and bleak and monochromatic day. Somewhat surreal. I held you all wrapped up as close as I possibly could.

I got out at 117 East Thirty-fifth Street, paid my share of the fare, said goodbye to your dad, and all by myself hauled everything up the three and a half flights of stairs to the safety and security of my home.

The apartment was warm and welcoming. Your crib in my bedroom was prepared. I laid you in that crib, with the beautiful linen that had belonged to your cousin Charlotte. The bumpers, quilt, sheets, and blanket received your little six-and-a-half-pound body, and there you slept. Everything was perfect. And to this day, it still is.

*Mothers Day, 2010*

*My father, Dennis Maxwell in his prime.*

# Step into My Office

"I can tell by the look on your face that you don't agree with anything I'm saying."

I sat rigidly on the brown couch in my father's brown study. He was at his desk smoking one cigarette after the next, stubbing them out, reclining cross-legged in his desk chair looking off into space. His presence was formidable.

It seemed like hours had passed since I had heard those most feared words: "Elizabeth, step into my office."

*NOW WHAT?*

My mother, who had been dutifully cleaning up in the kitchen, would dry her hands on the dish towel and then, with little heart for any of it, come and join us, sitting in a chair diagonally across from me, head down, while my father hammered on.

"You know, Lisa, your mother and I are not pleased…"

Immediately upon hearing those words I would retreat into the safest place I could find, deep in my soul to protect myself from the ensuing barrage of criticism and disapproval that was about to be endlessly and mercilessly fired at me. I was already bruised and broken from the fact that I had heard it all a million times before.

It was one long, harsh drone. "What is wrong with you? You're not doing this … blah blah… you're not doing that… blah blah…you have to get your head on straight … blah blah blah blah blah… you have bad hands."

I sat with those hands wedged between my thighs, looking down, silently challenging everything he said in my mind.

*But… but… NOOO!! That's not fair! That's not true, you're wrong!! Why are you so mean? I hate you!!* I would scream to myself.

These brutal critique sessions occurred more times than I care to remember over my childhood and into my teens. They were unrelenting. Perhaps, though, the cruelest punishment of all was listening to my mother saying absolutely nothing.

*734 North Cochran St., Charlotte, Michigan. Our house and the yard.*

# The Incinerator

"Thirteen, fourteen, fifteen ... "

The heat from the incinerator radiated out into the dark, dank, spooky basement. A bare bulb somewhere overhead was not bright enough to light the area. This iron, stove-like, gas-fired, scary thing would roar when fully engulfed. I learned later that it was a defunct coal furnace that my father used to burn trash. He was very resourceful.

My sister Linda and I stood dutifully by, arms at our sides, watching with eyes transfixed as the flames licked out of the top. I was not quite as tall as the frightful oven, she, tall enough to have her face freakishly lit by the orange light, craned to look in as each scrap of paper disappeared forever into the flames.

"Don't get too close; keep your hands away from here," my father would say, looming over us, so tall his upper body disappeared into the darkness. He rummaged through the brown paper shopping bag, removing each piece of combustible garbage that Linda and I had collected and dropping it into the inferno.

"Twenty-three, twenty-four, twenty-five ... "

One cent per piece split between us would yield maybe a quarter or fifty cents on top of our twenty-five cents a week allowance. That was huge.

We were being paid for cleaning up our yard. We lived on the main street in Charlotte, Michigan, just outside town in a tidy residential area. The Victorian house we lived in was set back from the road, with yards on every side. With careful searching we could find rather substantial bootie: wrappers, newspapers, cardboard, mud-encased, mysterious pieces of this and that. Somewhat of a treasure hunt was how we looked at it.

We would scour our yard for anything paper, even go down the hill and into our neighbors backyard, testing our bravery more on each expedition, we crossed the invisible property line, praying not to be challenged. Sometimes we would tear larger pieces in two, hoping Dad would not notice that the halves matched so we could double our number and make a little more money.

"Thirty-two, thirty-three ... "

He held the bag too high for me to see how many pieces were left. The anticipation was excruciating. Linda stood patiently, silently repeating the numbers in her brain, like me.

"Okay, well, it looks like forty-nine, but that's not an even number, so we'll make it twenty-four cents each. Okay, girls?"

"Okay, Dad," we said, knowing the math was off.

With his huge hands he would root around in his pockets, and out would come a pile of nickels, dimes, and quarters. The pennies were always separated beforehand, and had been deposited in his penny jar on his bureau.

"Let's see; here's two dimes and four nickels, that's not right. Here we go, one quarter a dime and two nickels. I'll have to get the pennies from upstairs. Well, that's alright."

I'd cup my hands, and he would drop the coins into them, leaving it to Linda and me to do the divvying up, I usually being the one to get short-changed.

By then, the fire in the incinerator had died down and was low and safe enough for me, to look into on my tiptoes. It was just a glowing orange light now. It was over, and it was always anticlimactic.

My father would unceremoniously shut the top, and we would wind our way through the basement, up the stairs, back into the kitchen. I relished rolling the warm coins in my pockets. (He would make good on the missing three cents later that day).

My mother would have happily handed us the extra money. Just because. No strings attached. But she had no say the family finances.

Setting out on what was fundamentally an adventure for my sister and me turned out to be a great life lesson. The random garbage we found put a few extra hard-earned coins into our pockets. The real payoff however, was a reward for our resourcefulness, to be repeated again and again throughout our self-supporting lives.

*My sister Linda, (left) and me in our yard in Michigan.*

*My sister Linda (rght) and me at the beach, best friends today.*

*Me (left), and my sisters Linda and Anne in our Sunday best, Michigan circa 1959.*

# Born Atheist

We moved from Weston, Connecticut to Charlotte, Michigan when I was three. We attended church every Sunday. We were Episcopalians, whatever that meant. My siblings and I attended Sunday school until we were old enough to be allowed into the grown up service. It was a ritual and we always dressed in our Sunday best. My two sisters and I usually wore matching outfits, hats, gloves, uncomfortable tights.

We filed into the church, sat on the hard creaky pews and I daydreamed. I was totally confused by whatever was being said, or dictated or foisted upon us. I understood enough, however, to know I wasn't buying any of it. Too dictatorial, too one-sided

I sort of liked the music. But it was never in my key, or anyone else's for that matter. It was either too high or too low. And those words:

"God this and Jesus that." *Who were those guys??*

Then there were the prayers:

"Our Father…" *I have a father!*

"Art in heaven…" *Did they have painting classes up there?*

"Howled be thy name…" *Why was he howling? It made no sense.*

To say I was skeptical was putting it mildly. Nothing stuck, except for a couple of the tunes. "Ode to Joy" and "Amazing Grace", were the ones my mom liked, and she sang them beautifully.

We moved back to Connecticut when I was in the sixth grade. Our family took a hiatus from attending church that year. Things were in a flux. We were living in a rented house in Westport for the year, then settled back into Weston as I entered the seventh grade. We became members of The Church of Emanuel. I don't recall going very often, but the subject of my Confirmation kept coming up.

In the meantime, I was learning about Buddhism in school, and found it fascinating. I simply could not understand how it was possible that we Episcopalians, or Christians or whatever we were could presume that our God was the only God; or that He was better than any other God. My issue wasn't so much about the religious tenets–I subscribed to the Golden Rule, and the Ten Commandments. But it seemed to me that everyone was thinking that their God was The One and no one else's.

So who was right? Well, in my opinion, clearly everyone, and no one.

"Confirmation classes start next week, honey," my mom said.

"I don't want to get confirmed mom."

"Come on Lizzy. It's important."

I bristled.

We negotiated, something my mom was really quite good at.

"Okay mom, I'll go to one class, but if I don't like it I'm not going to continue." I did feel it was important to keep an open mind since we hadn't been to church in a while, and I trusted that my mom would respect my position.

The week passed, the day arrived. We drove up to the picture-perfect white-steepled New England Church set back from the picture-perfect stone wall on a picture-perfect Fall day. A small sign pointed to a side door which led to stairs and to a basement room.

Most of the kids were a year or two younger than me, due to our non-attending church year in Westport. Being a year older was already an issue for me.

The Confirmation instructor was a middle-aged nondescript man who immediately gestured for me to take a seat in front of a stack of study materials. I looked at the books suspiciously.

"We are here to learn about our God, The Christian God, the only God." he began.

What the..?

That was it. I instantly started to challenge him.

I glared at him and said "What about the Buddhist God?" He was not pleased. I did not let up for a moment challenging practically everything he had to say for the entire class. When it was finally over, he made it clear he was very happy to see me go.

I stomped up the driveway. The sun had set. It was cold and dark and the dead leaves tumbled down ominously. The whole scene felt horrid.

Fuming, I plunked myself down on that cold stone wall and waited for my mom to pick me up. She was often late. She finally arrived, and pulled her car up near the wall. Solemnly, I got in and slammed the door. I crossed my arms, put my head down and said in no uncertain terms:

"I'm not going to get confirmed, and you can't make me." That was it.

She paused, and said, "OK". And off we went. She never brought it up again.

She kept her side of the bargain. That was like her.

*Emanuel Church, Weston, CT..*

*The quintessential day at the beach, Nantucket circa 1963.*

# The Goddess

"Come on Lizzy, let's go for a walk!"

"Okay mom." I brushed the sand stuck to my arms and legs and jumped up out of my post swim stupor, leaving my damp towel rumpled in the sand. My siblings, Anne, Linda and Gray were all lost in their own worlds in half-sleep states, oblivious. Everyone's hair was still wet and tangled from our salty swim.

The breeze danced around over my skin as clumps of sand continued to fall off the parts of my body I hadn't gotten to or cared about on the first attempt. Mom was wearing the same striped faded one-piece bathing suit she had worn the summer before and the summer before that.

The straps fell loose around her brown shoulders and she was carrying a small blue and white striped plastic beach bag. I trotted beside her, my eyes riveted to the sand, scanning every inch of the beach…side-stepping baby conch shell pods, fly-covered seaweed piles and driftwood.

The sky was blue gray in color, and the seagulls swooped all around in my peripheral vision. The smell of decaying sea matter wafted in the air. We were on our quest for the most perfect shells and pieces of sea glass. Heading into the sun, with squinted eyes I saw that as usual, there was not a soul in sight on our beach

"Look Little Bits!" her pet name for me, "Over there!" I studied the sand in the direction that her finger pointed and finally saw the beautiful bottle green gem poking out of the beach debris. I ran over and scooped it up.

"Thanks Mom. Ooohhh, it's beautiful!" I rubbed my fingers over the sea-smoothed edges, marveling at how much they had been softly worn over an unimaginable length of time. I held it up for her to see, and even though her Venus body was back lit, I could see her beaming smile. With pride, I dropped my gem into her bag. We walked about half an hour west, and half an hour back east. It was just the two of us, not talking much, delighting in the treasures we would find to add to our private personal collection. Our standards were equally high, not accepting anything the beach yielded that wasn't perfect.

It was our time alone together, and she was my goddess.

*My mother at Compo Beach, Westport, CT. 1949*

# *About the Authors*

**Gayle Gleckler** has had a successful career in advertising. She is currently the CEO, Creative Director of The Whole Enchilada Marketing Agency. As Executive VP Creative Director at Foote, Cone & Belding she created "I'm Gonna Wash that Gray Right Outta My Hair" for Clairol, then opened her own agency, Gleckler and Partners. Gayle co-wrote, and cast "The Lords of Flatbush", Sylvester Stallone and Henry Winkler's first movie. In 2010 Gayle co-wrote and illustrated a children's book, Milo, My Stray Cat. She began painting, collaborating with husband Tony Woolner. Art shows include: "In Plane View, Chinese New Year, Discovering Portugal, Exotic India, and in 2013 Out of Africa" in NYC. She considers her greatest creative success her son, Zachary Weiner. And now has a Motherhood bonus with her stepchildren David and Cookie Woolner. She received her Bachelor of Design from University of Florida, did graduate work at NYU and taught at School of Visual Arts.

**Eileen Grace** is a multimedia artist. She is an art teacher, a Connecticut resident since 1976 and currently lives and works in Weston.

A graduate of Marywood College is Scranton, PA, Eileen has studied with George Passantino of the New York Art Student's League, at Fairfield University and The Silvermine School of Art in Norwalk, Connecticut.

Since the crayon decoration of a freshly painted wall at the age of three, Eileen has been eager to paint on anything and everything. She has illustrated a children's book and done advertising illustrations for newspapers, brochures and magazines. A love affair with ceramics began in 1998 and now works in clay, hand formed and hand molded, carry the bright colors characteristic of Eileen's work. Elements of whimsy and humor are also part of her ceramic style.

She enjoys landscape painting in oils and watercolors and and has exhibited at the Westport Art Show, The Norfield Art Show, The Guilford Handcraft Center and the Burr Homestead show in Fairfield.

Eileen believes in creative schizophrenia. She looks forward to the continued exploration of the creative process in more and many media. Writing is her most recent endeavor. She is daughter of Clarissa, mother of Elizabeth, Christopher and Jason. Grandmother of Isabel and Finlay.

**Linda Howard Urbach**, a contributor to the Huffington Post is the author of *Madame Bovary's Daughter* (Random House Summer 2011). She is currently working on a new novel, *Sarah's Hair*, the story of Sarah Bernhardt's hairdresser. Two novels published by Putnam's (Under the name Linda U. Howard) *The Money Honey* and *Expecting Miracles* (Paramount owns movie rights). She co-authored with Roberto Mitrotti "The Secret Diary of Sigmund Freud" (20th Century Fox Specialized Film Division) and The Shoplifter. Her one act play "Scenes from A Cell" was a finalist in the 2002 New England One Act Festival. She taught creative writing at the Westport Writers Workshop and is the originator of "MoMoirs: The Umbilical Cord Stops Here!" a theatrical production in conjunction with Theatre Arts Workshop of Norwalk, She's also the creator of MoMoirs-Writing Workshops For and About Mothers. She is the mother of the one and only Charlotte Spring Clark.

**Lisa Maxwell** is an advertising art director, jazz singer, teacher, a wife, and (perhaps most proudly) a mom. A graduate of Parsons School of Design, Lisa started her career at Young & Rubicam and went on to work at many New York advertising agencies creating national ad campaigns for major advertisers, from Oil of Olay, to Campbell's Soup to Coca Cola. When first employed, she pursued training in jazz singing (her true love) while working full-time, and during that time appeared in cabarets in New York city for a span of 10 years. She also travelled extensively, both for work and personally. Highlights of her travels include summiting Mt. Kilimanjaro in 1986, a tour of Machu Picchu and the Galapagos Islands in 1987, and a stint in the Australian outback as a Jilleroo in 1988.

She had her son, Lake Wolosker as a single mom at age 37. In 1995, two months shy of her son's third birthday she met her husband George Newall.

She has since become an educator, continues freelance work as an art director, graphic and web designer and has produced two CD's of her jazz singing, in 2010 and 2011 respectively.

www.ingramcontent.com/pod-product-compliance
Lightning Source LLC
Chambersburg PA
CBHW061514050726
47593CB00002B/560